BREEDING SUCCESS

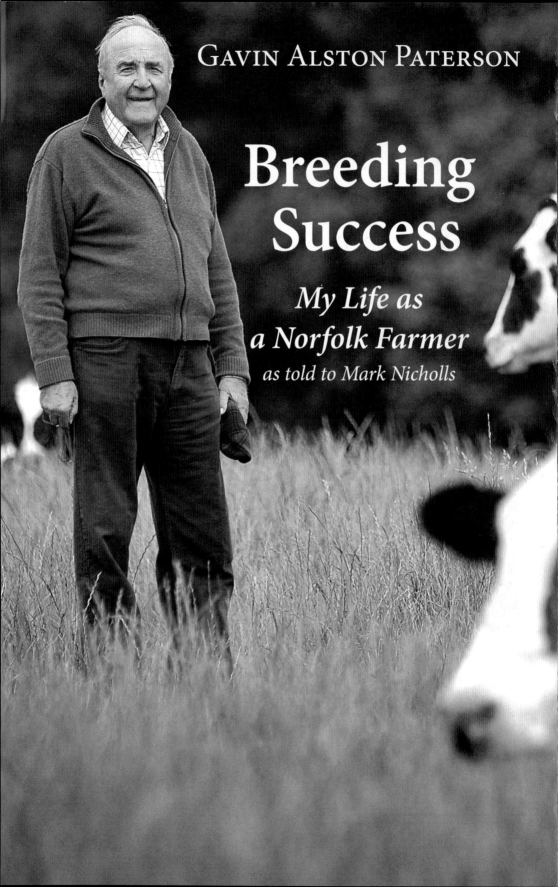

GAVIN ALSTON PATERSON

Breeding Success

My Life as a Norfolk Farmer

as told to Mark Nicholls

POPPYLAND
PUBLISHING

Picture credits

Eastern Daily Press /Antony Kelly: page 2
Gavin Paterson/Yellobric: page 164 (top and middle)
Christopher Pipe/Watermark: page 141 (bottom)
Poppyland Photos: page 43
James Robinson Images: front cover, pages 15, 100, 155, 161, back cover (bottom)
Other pictures are from the author's collection

'All that's needed to make good pasture is wild white clover and a Scotsman.'

For Marcia, Gavin, Alexander and Bruce – the next generation of Paterson family farmers

Gavin with his sons Gavin, Alexander and Bruce.
Top picture, left to right: *Alexander, Gavin, Marcia (author's wife), Gavin (the author), Bruce.*

6

CONTENTS

*James Andrew Paterson,
the author's father.*

*James Andrew Paterson
and his wife Marion.*

INTRODUCTION

My great grandfather Alexander Paterson was a master baker in East Kilbride, just south of Glasgow, and his wife was a Miss Lambie. The son they had, who was my grandfather, was John Paterson who moved to the farm at Torfoot, Drumclog, near Strathaven, as a boy. He was well-educated, respected and admired; he went to university after attending the local schools near Drumclog and Kilmarnock and as an adult and local farmer he spent much of his spare time helping those schools keep up to date with modern education methods. He was also invited to be Secretary and Treasurer of a local farmers group.

My father – James Andrew Paterson – was the son of John Paterson of Torfoot and his wife Susan Alston-Paterson. He was one of five children and while the farm they lived on was not that big, they also hired grassing areas. The family did most of the practical work but at difficult times could hire labour from labour letting and hiring events in Kilmarnock and those workers would live on the farm, staying in the 'bothy' above the cow shed or byre, which was a warm place in winter.

The family farmed a small herd of Ayrshire cows, perhaps 35, had a few sows and a contract to produce chicken eggs for hatchlings. Horses and ponies were the power to operate any machinery and also the transport to get to market. Milk was sold, or made into butter or cheese, which was also sold periodically in sales. I believe my grandmother Susan was in charge of that and very good at it. They were very thrifty and did not spend money if it was not necessary. When they went on holiday they visited relations at little cost, which was the family tradition. They could all milk and feed calves so if an emergency cropped up with illness or a birth, that was very handy and helpful.

This, however, brings me to explain just what inspired me to tell the story of my family, particularly my father's achievements, and some of our adventures, exploits, escapades and successes along the way.

I have to confess, I am not a great reader of books. By the time I have kept up with the agricultural news and paperwork I feel the rest of my time is better spent out on the farm keeping in touch with what is growing or seeing how the cows are. But I did read a book called *Breaking New Ground* by Alec Douet not so long ago. In fact I've read it twice. It is all about agriculture in Norfolk between 1914 and 1972, a period when father came to farm in Norfolk and I was growing up and beginning to listen to what was happening under my feet. I found I actually knew many of the people mentioned in it. For me, it did explain to some extent why some of the things that happened to our family could have happened and how that progress eventually changed Norfolk farming. That is one reason why I thought something should be written down about our family.

James Andrew Paterson, my father, moved down to Norfolk at a time when several other families from Scotland were heading south to settle in eastern England. They brought their farming practices, and their family traditions, with them and a desire to breed good dairy cows that produced a lot of milk. With that, and their grassland management techniques, they added a new dimension to farming in Norfolk, possibly even changed the face of it. They worked together, helped each other with ideas and advice, and became a strong and respected part of the farming community in Norfolk.

My father was an important part of that. He built up his farms, set out the way he wanted to farm and knew how to run a farming operation. He also knew what a good cow looked like and he shared those attributes, skills and knowledge with my brother Ian and me as we began to make our own way and livelihoods in farming. While Alec Douet's book was one reason behind my decision to tell the story of my father and our family as farmers in Norfolk, there is a second reason for sharing the tale with you. And that is simply the remarkable business life he had – from 70 acres on a small hillside in Drumclog to 3,000 acres on nice loamy land in east Norfolk.

GAVIN ALSTON
PATERSON
*Church Farm,
Smallburgh
April 2015*

*The daffodils glow on the side of the concrete
road on the estate (see page 84).*

Chapter One

PUNNETS OF
FRESH-PICKED RASPBERRIES

Gavin as a toddler.

The sun was shining. It always was; it was my childhood. They were warm, happy, days spent on and around the farm in those early years. The farmyard was always full of life with cows and pigs, busy with cowmen and boys and my favourite of all the animals, the horse. Our home, or the first home I really remember, was the Manor House at Worstead, which was a big red-brick house opposite the church and facing out onto the square. There was never much passing traffic, only the occasional clip-clop of a pony and trap used by farmers or dealers. We usually knew who was likely to be coming past long before they came into view because we could tell who the pony belonged to just by the sound and rhythm of the hooves. There was a big walled garden at Manor Farm and that was our playground. We had a three-wheeled tricycle and a little pedal car which we rattled around the garden in. There were places to run and hide and fruit and vegetables grew in abundance, certainly more than we could eat ourselves. My older brother Ian and I would pick the surplus fruit and fill a few punnets and then lug it around the cottages in a wicker basket, selling punnets to the cottagers for a few pennies. We were encouraged by our parents and I think it was a case of mother trying to get us to think about business at an early age. She might have given us some of the money from what we sold, I can't really remember; we did have pocket money but it was always more about us learning as well as using up the fruit we didn't need. We had punnets full of raspberries and strawberries, redcurrants, even a few blackcurrants, and we always did well. The tenants knew Ian and me and they were always happy to buy from us. The cottages weren't far away from the farm – they were mostly estate cottages – and we would always go to Honing Row. Mrs Bugg lived in one of these small flint cottages and I liked her a lot. She would have a punnet or two and always offered me a beaming smile whenever I knocked on her door; that is what I remember most fondly about her. I was grateful for that warm welcoming smile a few years later when I had to speak to her about another, more serious, matter.

The big garden was such a nice place. There were actually two gardens, and both were walled in. The second garden had a tennis court on it and there was a lovely summerhouse which you could sit in and watch the tennis. We were always told we must not go on the road and our parents knew we were quite safe to play as nippers in that garden; it was a lovely place for us, full of vegetables and flowers and the fruit we used to pick. There were wet days and we were probably inside when it rained but as often as we could we were outside playing. There were a lot of good days and there was always something going on and back then, in those warm, sunny summer days of the 1930s, despite whatever else was happening in the world, we had little to worry us or care about.

We had arrived at Manor Farm when I was about four years old. Ian, who was christened John but known by the Gaelic name of Ian, was born on 3 June 1927 and was three years older than I. He would have had clearer memories of our life before that in a farm at Rushall in the south of Norfolk, but I remember very little, if anything, of it. Father was a Scot and had arrived in Norfolk with a number of other Scottish farmers who had been lured south by the prospect of hiring a farm to work.

Before that, he worked on my grandmother's farm in Scotland. My grandfather was a respected landowner where the family came from but he had died quite young, at the age of 54, in 1909. Two of father's brothers also died at around the same time as my grandfather passed away. They were only 19 and 21. They must have been difficult times for my grandmother Susan who took on the management of the farm until her oldest son Robert took over. Over the next few years father helped Robert manage the farm while the younger brother, Cecil – who would also later move to Norfolk – took a job in a bank. They had good cows, good Ayrshires. It was in 1922 that father had been down to Norfolk on holiday with two friends and they had made up their minds that Norfolk was where they wanted to farm, though he did not particularly want to leave Scotland at that stage. Over the next couple of years or so he looked at more farms in Scotland, motorcycling all over the country to try to find a suitable farm but with little success; by the time he was 27 he was getting itchy feet and keen to start farming on his own. As time passed he realised there was more likelihood of getting a farm in Norfolk as it was becoming apparent the landlords in this part of England were not getting on well with their current tenants and were always keen to interview new people to move in. He also had two good friends and advisers, who had been farming successfully in East Anglia for a number of years: John Alston from Besthorpe Hall who came from Winkenfield, Darvel, and James Alston (1881–1958) whom we all knew as 'Uncle James'. He farmed at Uphall and was from Yondercroft. Uncle James, who had first settled in Suffolk in 1903 before moving to Uphall Farm at East Harling in 1911, was to become an important figure to father throughout his early farming life and, for that matter, quite a few other Scots who moved south. He was always willing to give advice and help and his was an opinion that was respected. I think it was generally felt that if Uncle James thought something was a good idea, then it generally was and a lot of people followed his advice. He was certainly the most influential of the Scottish farmers who moved down to Norfolk.

The farm father set his eye on was Hall Farm at Rushall, near Pulham St Mary Air Station, right next to where they used to tether the big airships. Father recalls two airships housed in huge sheds and it being 'quite an event' when they went away and came back. The R33 famously broke away from her mast during a gale one day and tore away her nose piece and drifted out over the North Sea with her crew on board, but father clearly remembers her being brought back safely the following day.

At first, he was not that struck on Rushall because it was full of bushes and parts of it were derelict. He actually thought it was not really worth bothering about but Uncle James advised him otherwise. So on 29 June 1925, a few days after marrying my mother Marion from Yondercroft, he took over the 256 acres of Rushall lock, stock and barrel, at a fortnight's notice, which saw him buy everything on the farm including 17 cows which were into milk production. He carried out the work Uncle James had advised, getting rid of the bushes and bringing the land into cultivation. Uncle James was not only prepared to offer advice, but he was supportive too and during father's first year at Rushall, he was a regular visitor to the farm. A moat ran around the farmhouse, taking drainage from the yard and surface water from the

Rushall farm in 2009.

land and acting as the water supply for cooling milk and washing purposes. All the domestic water was drawn from a well with a chain and pail until a bore was put down and water pumped by an engine.

And that is where I, Gavin Alston Paterson, came into this world on 16 May 1930.

The farm also had about 20 large black breeding sows and grew crops including barley, wheat, oats, beans, mangold, swedes and later sugar beet and there was a small acreage of grass. Horses did most of the work, though some of the hay stubbles and corn stubbles were cultivated up with traction engines. There would be one at each end of the field pulling the cultivator back and forward on a wire rope.

Father was an ambitious man and always wanted to succeed so he started to buy a few more cows, even though the local blacksmith – who was also the local carpenter – warned him against it.

'I've heard you are going to have 40 cows on that land,' the blacksmith remarked. 'That land'll never hold 40.' But before long, father was successfully herding 60 cows on the land. He just knew about cows and what he could do with them and that was the key to his success. The cows would not be that brilliant but they were there for milking and I believe I am right in saying that he increased the milk production even with no more cows calved. If you had 17 milking and you increased the amount of milk you were sending away with nothing extra calved that would simply be through good management. He would have known that they were good production cows anyway. That is why he was prepared to take them on. He had a labour team on the farm of about 12 and two boys and that included the cowmen, horseman and labourers.

Every farmer who came down from Scotland put a herd of cows on their land and that was the key to their success in my opinion. Not only did they produce milk but they also produced manure, making their land more fertile. But it wasn't just Scots who were moving in to Norfolk at that time, there were people from other parts of the country coming to Norfolk as well.

Father always had stories to tell from those days and one was about Dan Bunnett whom he found late one morning sitting down on the ground when he should have been picking potatoes.

'What's the matter Dan?' says father, to which Dan replied, 'I have broken my leg, sir, and have sent one of my kiddies home for my spare one.'

Dan worked mostly among the cows and stock and his artificial leg was no hindrance to him at all. His son Bertie also worked the farm and in fact worked for us for all his life. But cows were what father knew best and he would have learned how to manage cows on the farm in Scotland when working for his brother. He put that knowledge into action when he started to farm on his own, and he was successful with cattle from the outset. Alec Douet's excellent book *Breaking New Ground: Agriculture in Norfolk 1914–72* (Coldbath Books, 2012) mentions a number of the families that came down to Norfolk to settle and start farming in this area. It gives so much information about the land in Norfolk and how farming practices changed over much of the twentieth century.

In the years between World War One and World War Two, dairying grew in popularity in Norfolk, particularly as milk provided a regular income and bullock yards were being converted to accommodate cows. The migration of Scottish farmers to the county was a big factor in that growth and they took the lead in that respect. It was acknowledged that because of the low rainfall, good pastures were not easy to establish in Norfolk though as Douet confirms, 'the Scots were expert in grassland management'. There was a saying at the time that said 'all that was needed to make good pasture was wild white clover and a Scotsman'.

Father came from a farm of 70 acres in Lanarkshire in Scotland, which was so remote from what he ended up working in Norfolk but he was a very determined character. He was very direct, talked a lot of common sense and spoke with a broad Scottish accent in a strong, deep voice and when he said something, people listened. He was of average height and you never needed to wonder what he was thinking.

He had been doing farm work himself with his brother on the farm and he was always looking to learn how to get things done. At the time, many of the Norfolk farmers saw themselves as gentleman farmers and would not do the physical work. In the early part of the century there were two types of Norfolk farmers: those who were gentleman farmers and managed the farms and those who rolled up their sleeves and worked in the fields with their men. But what was clear in the years before World War One, and for some time thereafter, was that Norfolk's farm labourers, as Douet says, 'with few exceptions . . . were hard worked, poorly paid, and dismally housed'.

That attitude of the 'gentleman farmer' was part of the problem with Norfolk farming and why so much was going wrong. It was the fashion in Norfolk to say 'I am a gentleman farmer and I do not keep cows.' But with the Scots one of the main things that they did was to keep cows and when they came down here, they all wanted a herd of cows. That was a bit of a problem for the landlords at first because they had to spend money to supply accommodation for cows but father would not have taken a farm until the old bullock boxes were converted and he was able to put in a herd of cows. He had been a hands-on farmer; that changed to some extent because he was so busy but he always knew what he wanted the men to do and he always insisted they did exactly what he asked of them.

Before long, father began to look around to see how he could better himself and about four years after taking on Rushall he took over the adjoining farm, Bethel Farm. Better known by the locals for some reason as Starve Acre, it had 71 acres of heavy land. But things were difficult in farming, particularly those farms where the land was heavy, and landlords found they were no longer easy to let. A further four miles on from Rushall, there was a farm called White House Farm at Pulham Market which was 319 acres and the tenant had retired. The agent wrote to father asking him to look at White House too and was offering it at a low rent, so father took it. Rentals were cheap at the time. In the 1920s rentals fell and fell and by 1933 they were at, or even below, the levels of the First World War, and a growing number of estates were also coming up for sale.

But something else was going on too. In the meantime, father had been up to the Worstead area to see his brother-in-law James Alston, my mother's brother, who had similarly decamped from Scotland and was farming in Sloley. Father had a keen eye and didn't miss much on the land and as it happened on the day he was up there in east Norfolk, there were horses and a plough working in a field next door. Father immediately noted the quality of the land and how it appeared to be so much easier to work than the land he was working at Rushall. He knew then that this was where he wanted to be and he left his brother-in-law with the view that if some land or a farm came up in that area to let, he would be interested. Literally a week or two after taking on White House he got a call from his brother-in-law saying the very farm near where he had been looking was up for let. This put father into something of a quandary, as he already had plenty of land to manage. He was undecided and spent some time thinking it through but finished up hiring Manor Farm, Worstead, which was 412 acres at the time, for entry the following Michaelmas, 11 October 1932.

Manor Farm was right in the middle of the village with the farm house facing on to the square opposite the Church of St Mary. Father was a Scottish Presbyterian but he would say to us that he liked living opposite the church because he could hear the service from where he was. We had to go to church though. It was traditional that if you were farming in the parish you would get a box pew and when you hired a farm you could expect stipulations that you attend the parish church and support it. St Mary's had, and still has, box pews. I wasn't that old but soon discovered that while the vicar was doing his sermon you could sit there in a certain position and he could not see you and you could not see him. You were out of the glare so if you misbehaved you did not upset the vicar; but I am sure we did not misbehave all the time.

Manor Farm needed some work doing on it before it was suited to father's

An early photograph of the Manor House, Worstead.

needs and he asked the landlord to convert some bullock boxes into a cowshed. Bullock boxes were used in those days to fatten the bullocks but father didn't want to keep cattle for meat. It was a wise move in those difficult days. Grain prices were falling and Norfolk farmers were not getting good returns on cattle and sheep. Father's thoughts were on milk production, and that was what he knew. He had been brought up on milk production and egg production and that was important to him as it would bring in an income each month. It was the very foundation of his thinking.

'You can only fatten a bullock once,' he would say.

The landlord had the inside of the cattle shed stripped out and made stalls for the cows to stand and put a feeding trough and water bowl at the front and a gutter at the back so the urine outfall could get away but there was still the muck to cart, which was one of the jobs the old Norfolk farmers of the day weren't that keen on. Cows created a lot of dirt in the farmyard but the attitude of father, and the other Scots who moved down, was quite different from that of the local farmers. He knew how to manage the dirt from cows as he had done it for most of his life. The key was to put it back on the land and improve fertility because putting manure on the land is how you get better crops.

The original Scottish farmers that came down had a good reputation and were successful, so when you get the landlords beginning to see they could make it a success, they would look for more of those people to take on the farms because they were not only able to look after the farms but they could pay the rent as well. My father was always so lucky with the things that happened, he was always thinking and looking ahead. In those days farmers were struggling and some were having difficulty paying their rent and sometimes they just had to pack up.

Father began to set things up at Manor Farm; he was bringing in calf heifers and getting them served ready to calf, and getting in the staff he needed. But while father had found the farm he was looking for at Worstead, he had put himself in a tricky position because his farms at Rushall and White House were some 30 miles from Worstead. I imagine these were some of his most difficult times in farming because he had so much land to look after, as well as the cows, and some of it at the other end of the county. The telephone was his only form of contact and he said there was nothing worse than leaving one end with everything working all right and then getting a telephone call saying that things had gone wrong and he was needed back there at Rushall to sort it out.

'That was a quite impossible situation that I should not have let myself be put in,' he told me when I was older, but he managed and when the cowsheds were ready at Worstead he had his herd walked all the way from Rushall, 30 miles into east Norfolk, with none of them the worse for their journey.

Worstead Manor House was a large house and was rented with the farm. It had a lot of big rooms and needed several fires to heat the house on colder days. While it has been altered over the years, and was originally two houses, parts of it were old, very old in fact, and may even date from the fifteenth century. Father and mother's bedroom had a dressing room with it, and there were two or three other bedrooms and I shared a room with my brother which overlooked the road running into the square. It was a tall, old house with a weaving loft, which was common with Worstead having been a weaving village. The weaving loft was a big room with a clear floor and a small office in the corner and there may have been a dozen or so looms up there at one stage. There would be a supervisor who would sit in the office with a glass front and watch the weaving going on but that was all gone by the time we lived there. What was known as the 'underneath' drawing room, because it was under the weaving loft, is where guests would sit if they came to visit and that was something that happened all the time. It had a great fireplace in it and seats either side.

There were always visitors to the house. People like father, who had come down from Scotland, would meet and talk and would be helpful to each other. Many Sundays we had company or we would go out somewhere and visit. This was a huge help to people who did not know the system of working in Norfolk, they had all sorts of problems but would sit around and talk about them and between them they would get them solved. As I grew up I listened to those conversations. It was like another education to me. I would be sitting and listening and people would say they were having trouble with such and such a problem and there would be perhaps three or four others who would say they had the same thing and between them they would know somebody who could solve it. You have to remember that this was in the time of horses, and that is where some of the problems were, with illness in the horses or the cattle. The Scottish farmers talked to each other about this and I was growing up in that atmosphere. There was always someone who knew about something and they were not afraid to talk about it. An awful lot of farmers do not want to talk about their problems or tell other people they have a problem but I think their minds must have been thinking different in as much as they knew about things and could talk about their experiences and take advice and that would be a good thing to do. Technically, they were away from home and they had to learn local habits. I remember dad talking about what he had seen and learning to do certain things in a certain way because that was the habit of the district. My early lessons in farming were learned on the hearth. These conversations were always constructive, they were never pointless, there was always something someone wanted to know the answer to and I did not stop learning the whole time about what went on down on the farm and that was probably what my parents intended.

The Scots were all trying to 'do different' at a time that Norfolk did not 'do different'. Families such as the Patersons, the Alstons and the Cargills, which came from the north of Scotland, all knew each other or had some contact and there were several other families that came down as well and I can understand families following each other down. That was as much to do with what was happening in Norfolk as with what was happening in Scotland. Some of that was because let farms were available at a time that landlords in Norfolk were not getting the rent they were expecting, while in Scotland there were not so many farms available but there were farmers with sons that were looking to go somewhere else and looking for somewhere different to farm. The Scots brought with them a desire to succeed but also knowledge of dairy farming.

Douet sums up the Scots perfectly: 'Although most started with little capital, they managed, by concentrating on dairying, by sound management and close financial control, and by sheer hard graft, to expand their operations in the difficult times. Many started on poor land but gradually moved to better. It was mainly due to the Scottish families who came to Norfolk in the 1920s and 1930s – Alston, Cargill, Cranford, Drummond, Lang, Laurie, Mailer, Mitchell, Paterson and Ritchie, as well as those who came from the west country like the Kidners and Joe Wyatt, that, by 1938, Norfolk had become a major milk producing county.'

Milking herds grew and James Alston (Uncle James) was described by Douet as 'perhaps the county's leading dairy farmer' and was milking 240 cows in 1931 compared to 70 in 1924. British Friesians were also growing in popularity at the time, and in the early 1930s about 20% of the county herds were Friesian, another 20% were Norfolk's own indigenous dual-purpose cow the Red Poll but the remainder were made of a mix of breeds. (Today, my son Alexander still has a small herd of Red Poll, which he keeps on Worstead Park.)

Hard graft and a desire to expand his farming operations were on father's mind,

Red Poll cattle, Worstead Park.

but there was always that willingness to share knowledge and help each other out. Sunday afternoons for us was about friends and social gatherings, about learning and needing to know answers to problems. Most Sundays, with mother and father expecting guests and families of farmers coming for afternoon tea, mother would get the family dressed up. I do remember one such time that my brother asked me if I had seen the little piglets in the farmyard. You could go from the house at Worstead and into the back of the farmyard where there was an open fronted shed. Ian said to me the little pigs were in that shed so we opened the door and all we could see was a blooming great sow with all the little pigs under the straw asleep. My brother had already seen them before and he was keen to show them to me. I would have been four or five years old and we thought the little pigs were so exciting. We went into the shed and quickly stirred the sow and little pigs up and the whole place began to move. The little pigs shrieked and then the big sow came and knocked me down and left me with a cut on my brow. I tailed off back indoors and got a dressing down from my mother for getting untidy and also a telling off that we should not have been anywhere near the sow. What we learned that day was that you do not play around with an old sow with a lot of piglets.

Gradually we discovered more about what was going on with the farm and started to take an interest as we got to know people better. As well as these conversations I listened into, the people who were working on the farm were always interested in talking to us. Some of them talked to us more than others but they were mostly pleased to see us and to explain what they were doing. One thing I can remember in those days is that everybody thought about safety and if you were doing something you shouldn't be doing the men would come and tell you straight away.

Family life in the house was lived to a fairly strict routine. Father was always an early bird, he would be out on the farm early in the morning and I followed the same thing. Father was running the farm or had meetings to go to while mother ran the house. It was not just the family that was there, we had people round the house working with the chickens or in the garden. In those days we had a handyman called Billy Knock who did all the jobs around the house and we got on very well with him. He was the man who did the chickens, was the gardener and drove the cars if needed. He lived on the farm but was outside the labour force of the farm. The chickens were mother's department. She managed the eggs, had them cleaned and put in boxes ready for collection. Mother was also involved in a lot of the detail of the farm management, taking messages and listening out for telephone calls. We also had a washerwoman who came in once a week and she was one of our babysitters as well. Her name was Mrs Howard and she used to tell us funny stories about the village and about all sorts of other things. We also had a maid when I was younger, and I remember seeing an old photograph of her in her maid's uniform. Her name was Ethel and Ian would have remembered her better because by that time he was eight or nine and she used to help him with his homework. She was also the one who would clear out the fireplaces, make them ready and light them and that was a lot of work because in a normal house there would be a lot of fireplaces, two or three upstairs and some downstairs to heat the whole house.

Beyond the farmyard and our walled garden, I remember the square very well. There were shops all around: Mr Copping sold fruit, vegetables and other produce for the cottages, then there was the Post Office which was also a shop that seemed to sell everything, it was a little round shop at the bottom of the square, and to the left of that was the bakery, run by Mr Grimes the baker. Mr Norgate was the butcher and he was across the road from the Manor House on the other corner. There were delivery boys on bikes with big baskets on the front and you could always hear if there was a pony and cart coming from a long way away with the clip-clop sounds.

Harry Yaxley was the blacksmith and I knew him quite well because one of the jobs the farm boys did was to take the horses to the blacksmith's shop because someone had to be there with the horse to shoe it and it wasn't really a man's job, though actually us boys didn't do that much to help. He had a forge and maybe two stalls for the horses at the other end of the forge. He was a really solid character and I was often down there with the horses. Some of the horses would lose their shoes in quite a short time while others would keep them longer but they had to be shod ready for the heavy work so we always tried to time it so that they were shod again for the spring work.

My younger sister, Marion, was born at Worstead on 20 August 1934. We had a resident nurse who came and lived in with us. I remember one day the nurse shouting out of the bedroom window down to my father that he had a daughter. He was known to say after her birth 'that was the best harvest I ever had' and it was a remark he made often because there were not many daughters in the family and even today there are still not many girls. Nurse Hunt retired onto the Worstead estate after father found her one of the small cottages to live in. That suited them and her because she became one of our babysitters.

Nurse Hunt was a stickler, and when we were youngsters she was very corrective if we did anything wrong in speech or actions: if we did not say words properly she would correct us, not that it had much effect. She was strict and as a result she did not become my favourite person even though she was probably right and she was doing it to try to keep us speaking correctly as youngsters. Interestingly, my parents did not complain about her. Our parents spoke with a Scottish twang and we were beginning to speak with a Norfolk twang and within that she was trying to get us to speak English correctly. Nurse Hunt was always there in our early years and, despite her strictness, with the three of us children in the world and a busy farm full of cows and horses and a big safe garden to play in, my childhood was nothing but a happy one.

Chapter Two

A Farm Favourite

They were big, heavy and strong. They were our horses and were the powerhouse of the farm when I was a boy. If I remember rightly we had eight of them in the Worstead stable, though father did own a tractor by that stage. He had bought his first tractor as early as the autumn of 1932 when he was still farming at Rushall and it was Bertie Bunnett who drove it, but the horses still dominated the farm environment. Bertie was a very strong man and he'd made it his business to get to know about tractors before a lot of other people did. After ploughing land at Rushall, the tractor came to Worstead with Bertie driving it and cultivating the stubbles on Manor Farm. The tractor helped father a lot when he moved to Worstead as the land was foul with twitch and other rubbish. At about this time, deep ploughing came into fashion so with Bertie behind the wheel, the tractor was used to good benefit. It soon became apparent that the cheapest way to clean land was to deep plough it and put the rubbish to the bottom.

Bertie was Dan Bunnett's son and I knew him well because I had grown up with him. When he came up to Worstead with the tractor he stayed in one of the cottages at Honing Row. Having the tractor here was a big help and once the harvest was over we could get stuck in to cultivating the land ready to get started with the drill. But while the tractor did a lot of work and created a lot of interest, we were still very much living in the horse world and they did much of the work on the farm for many years after that. Everyone knew the horse was slow but they did have advantages; they didn't flatten the land like the tractor tyres did, for example, and the old horsemen were wonderful wise old boys. They knew the answers to most of the problems but that was something that you had to learn, you couldn't just go to school and pick it up.

From as young as I can remember, the horses were my favourites on the farm, they were my first love. I used to lead them home when we turned them out to grass in the summertime and I found I always had a favourite mare which was a horse

Young Gavin with horse Floborough Monarch.

that was reliable, didn't have bad habits and was usually the quietest in the stable. At Worstead we had Suffolk Punch. Father had been used to Clydesdales in Scotland but he chose Suffolk Punch because they always had 'good clean legs', as he'd say. Some horses can develop problems with their legs – known as 'greasy legs' – but the Suffolk Punch was always a good horse. With horses there would be a 'hold-yea' boy who would sit on a horse's back if you were filling a wagon with sheaves of corn. The boy's job was to move the wagon on when required instead of a man going out in front to lead it on. That was a job I liked doing and I'd climb up the shaft of the wagon and on to their backs and into position. We would get up early and turn up on our bikes or go out with the horsemen but we had to be careful and we learned quickly of the dangers. We knew which horses were safe and which ones you did not play about with. One of the jobs I recall is with the old horse-driven wooden elevator. The horse went round and round underneath the elevator and had to be kept going and at times that was my job to see that it did just that. In the stable of eight, sometimes nine, horses there would be several geldings and one or two

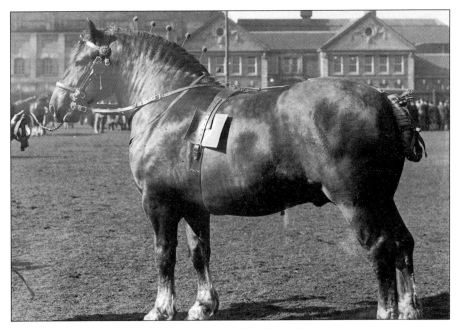

Worstead Prince, a pure-bred Suffolk Punch farm horse.

mares. Across the farm we would have several mares that we would breed every year. They were good horses but looking after them was labour intensive and at Worstead we had 18 men in the stable, including the boys. The farmyard was alive, there were more men on the farm than at any time I can remember and the cows created a lot of activity too but horses were the power implement and they were my favourite. At the beginning, I got to ride on the horse's back and that suited me down to the ground. But as boys we also needed to learn about them too. If you put your foot in front of a horse and it puts its foot on yours, you did not do that twice. It hurt. I had to understand what the horses were like and would get to know the horses; the ones that were flighty and the ones that were dead quiet. The old stable at Worstead is still there but it has now been made into a house.

Father, of course, was more interested in the cows and it wasn't long before we began to learn more about the herds. There were 72 cows in the herd. That was father's idea of the right number for a herd which so many men could handle. I used to play in the farmyard and would go down to the cowshed and see the milking and help feed the calves and most of the men were pleased to see me. There were always boys about the place and if they wanted a job on the farm, they had to learn about what went on, just as I was going to have to do. These were boys from the village too and I used to play with them. We used to go bird nesting to see if there were any eggs or young in the nests. It is not something you would do nowadays but it helped us learn the ways of the countryside.

We were hand milking the cows in those days and I used to go across there when I was a small boy and watch the milking in the cowshed at Manor Farm and I would be encouraged to have a go. I would often go back to the house with a jug of milk if we needed some. There were always plenty of calves about and I soon knew what was going on with the farm as I was always around the place.

The cow men would start at around 5am and the first thing they would do would be to feed the cows and milk them. The cows were kept in stalls with a trough and water bowl and milking them by hand was a time-consuming job but a man could milk 10 cows twice a day. I imagine there would be about seven men to the herd and if you watched a good milker, my goodness he pulled the milk out of the cows. Nowadays, it is so much easier with cows milked twice a day by machine. Not everybody was gifted in this but there definitely was a technique; it was about squeezing with your hand and manipulating with your fingers. When the men worked the udders by hand they would make sure there was no mastitis and the head herdsman also had to go round and check that the cows were milked properly because if they were not milked properly there could be problems. There were always the calves to feed as well.

We had our own lorries to cart our milk to the dairy. Everything was recorded in the milk book with the milk lorry driver having to fill it in and record the amount he had picked up because it was that figure that would determine how much we were paid. Those figures were the key to an awful lot of the business. After the cows were milked, there was still a lot of work to do before the milk was ready to be taken away. It had to be cooled for a start. We milked into buckets and would tip that into a bigger bucket and take it round to our dairy to be cooled. Those big buckets of milk were heavy and taking them round to the dairy was a big job. The man would lift the milk up the steps and tip it into the top of the cooler, which was a big dish which would take a bucket quite easily. The cooler was a double metal corrugated sheet with water running through the inside and milk on the outside and that is how it was cooled. Underneath the corrugation, the milk would run into churns and you would put a lid on the 10 gallon churn when it was full. At the bottom there were three spouts and under each spout you could plug each one while you wheeled a full churn out of the way and put an empty one in its place. Then these churns were lifted up about three feet onto a platform and wheeled through a door to the outside and from there lifted onto the back of our lorry and driven to the Co-op Dairy.

We knew the manager of the Co-op Dairy, Mr John Robertson. He was a Scot and was always hammering on father's door because they wanted more TB-free milk and father could provide that. Norfolk was one of the first places that started to test for TB-free cattle and then that moved further into the east of England and other parts of the country until it reached the west of England where it all seemed to stop. Badgers could spread the disease to cattle so badger culling was used to try to stop that and it worked well but it annoys me immensely that they did not finish the job off in the south west. That was just to do with people complaining that it would kill all the badgers but there were a lot of badgers that were TB-free as well so it wouldn't have affected the badger population as badly as people thought it might. Father's milk was free of tuberculosis and most of it would end up in schools and playgroups in Norfolk in those small bottles that were a third of a pint. We had a job to supply the schools but the work became very important as the dairy wouldn't deliver any milk unless they knew it was TB-free. Father had a huge milk operation and we had good staff to do the job.

As well as the horses, chickens and cattle, the farm grew quite a few different crops: sugar beet, potatoes and wheat and barley on rotation. We also had fields of peas and beans but father's key to his success was that he would get a cheque every month for milk and eggs. My father used to say that a good cow, and milking well, was a big asset. He had also been brought up in Scotland where the farming system involved the family. If they were short of labour the women worked and often the

Looking after the workers: staff Christmas party.

cows were milked by women. In fact, the whole family worked on the farm. Much of his thinking was shaped by his upbringing in Scotland and later influenced by what the other Scottish farmers in Norfolk were doing.

Father was a workaholic. When he grew up, he was doing all the practical work on the farm back in Scotland and his theory was that if you were a farmer with work that would bring in a monthly return, the bank manager would be much more pleased to see you. That also meant you were in a position to borrow money if you wanted but you did not borrow money if you did not need to. All that I did know was that father had principles and he would always follow them. He knew that in those days nobody really had much money and that included the farm workers. His motto was that 'if you get a good man, you would do something to help his family and especially his wife and you would make him a long-term prospect'. Working staff moved on a lot in those days, either because the boss sacked them or they did not like the boss, so when he found a good man he would do whatever he could to keep him. And that generally meant providing them with a nice place to live. Most of our men had quite big families so they were looking for a good job with good money and regular work. What I remember about their houses is that the gardens these men kept were immaculate, they had as much in their gardens as they could grow and if you gave them a brace of rabbits to eat with what they grew they would be highly delighted.

Proud cottage tenants: head horseman Dan Chapman
and Mrs Chapman and garden produce.

During this time, father expanded. Not long after coming to Worstead he hired Crostwight Hall Farm which had 476 acres of land and was about four miles nearer the coast than Manor Farm. He thought Crostwight a very good farm and his thinking was to give up Rushall and White House and move the stock from them to Crostwight, including the cows from Rushall. When he left Rushall, it was taken over by his younger brother Cecil. At Michaelmas 1935, he hired Manor Farm, Dilham, which had 416 acres of land and joined the Worstead Farm on the same estate. I remember how father first came to rent the land on the estate. He was looking at his cows one night when the landlord came by, riding his horse, and stopped to have a chat. He related to father how the tenant from Dilham Manor could not pay his rent and told my father that if he were to hire it, he would be pleased. With that in mind, father thought it through and took it on, at the same time giving up Crostwight to my uncle Rob Alston who also had land at Witton next door.

Writing in later life about Manor Farm, Dilham, father recalled, 'this I thought the best farm I had got, no dairy on it, but again buildings were converted to stall 72 cows and quite a number of heifers were bought at Lanark.' He paid between £13 and £28 for the Ayrshires.

The hired land at Dilham was added to what he had bought in 1934 – that was Lodge and Ivy Farms at Dilham of 107 acres and 86.5 acres. Father had bought that land with a modest inheritance, which was quite unusual because in those early days most Scots were tenants. In fact, when he went into Norwich the following week he saw Uncle James, who was his adviser and supporter but on this occasion told father, 'You don't buy land. You can't get your money out if there's a collapse.'

I loved being on the farm in those days, seeing the horses, watching the milking and learning about what was going on, but I also had to go to school before long. I began to grow but not like my older brother. Ian was big and heavier than me, he was chunky and I remember being skinnier than he was. I was not very robust at an early age. I was about four or five years old when I first went to school, a private school in North Walsham, and while I do not recall much about it I do remember one of the teachers and his wife, Mr and Mrs Godfrey. They were both very good to me. Mrs Godfrey was a real Irish lady, a wonderful lady, and he was a nice man as well but she had a sparkle about her which made her quite different. They would try to get me to listen to what they were saying. And I did, I paid attention to them. Mr Godfrey had played cricket in his younger days, most likely at a high level, and he wanted to teach us boys how to play. We went to a field near the school and he set up the wickets but he also set up a door which he put behind the wicket so we did not have to run too far to fetch the ball. He would do the bowling and one of us had to sit behind the door and wait until the ball came and then pop up and send it back. One day, I looked up too soon and the ball hit me between the eyes and knocked me out. I can recall that Mr Godfrey's face was pretty serious when I came round. He was carrying me back to the school but he brightened up when he saw I was all right because he was worried that I had been seriously hurt. But cricket was never my thing after that.

We spent our early school days at the private school and were due to move to another school in North Walsham but when the war broke out we were sent up to Scotland. We had been up to Scotland quite a bit for our holidays as children and we also used to have outings, not so much seaside holidays, but we would go to the coast to places like Cromer and Blakeney, though Scotland is where we went the most. Perhaps I was not too aware of what was happening in the world outside the farm, I was happy and enjoying life but my parents – and most of their Scottish friends – were worried. They were worried about what was happening in Europe as Germany began to take over other countries. I did not necessarily appreciate it, or understand the consequences and implications, but while the sun may have been shining there were storm clouds of a different nature on the horizon, the threat of war. Eventually, on 3 September 1939, that day arrived and Britain and Germany found themselves at war again.

I recall now that there was one time, just as the war was starting, that a new family were coming down from Scotland to start farming in Norfolk. The plan was that they would arrive at Manor Farm House and stay the night with us before they went to their new farm at Skeyton. Mother and father were expecting them at about 5pm, and Ian and I were very excited about seeing them arrive. However, time got on and it was six o' clock and then seven o'clock. It must have got a bit later because we were sent to bed. When they eventually arrived, it must have been gone eight o'clock at night. Ian and I were still awake though, we were too excited to sleep, and we stood at the top of the staircase in the farm house when we heard them come in and waved at them, though we were soon sent back to bed. It turned out they had got lost, which thinking about it wasn't that difficult to do at that time in Norfolk. There was this uneasy feeling that if the Germans were going to invade, they'd come in through Norfolk, so to confuse the Germans if they did land here, all the road signs had been removed. It was okay for people who knew where they were going but strangers arriving in the county didn't stand a chance of finding their way around.

Soon after that, life changed for us. The war can't have been going on for that long before father, and the other Scottish farming families who had moved to Norfolk, began to talk about the risks. They had all clearly talked it through amongst themselves and the upshot of it was that they felt that for us young children, it was better not to be in Norfolk at that time because of the dangers they foresaw with the war. The consensus was that it was safer for the children to go back to Scotland. They were genuinely concerned that Hitler would invade England and Norfolk would be one of the first places where the Germans would land. So one day, we found ourselves at North Walsham railway station; mother, Ian, my sister and I standing on the platform with a number of other families and friends, people who had moved to Norfolk from Scotland. They were those who we saw often or were regular Sunday afternoon visitors to our home in Worstead. We said our goodbyes and caught the train for the long journey to Scotland with a group of other Scottish families who were making their way north. We had no idea how long we would be away for but my parents were extremely concerned for our welfare and believed that it was too dangerous for us to stay in Norfolk. They were fearful of what the war would bring and when it would end. I didn't know it at the time, but as we left North Walsham on the train, a friend of my father's turned to him and said: 'You know, Jimmy, we may never see them again.'

The Paterson family: James, Ian, Marion, Gavin, Marion (also known as May).

Chapter Three

Is Hitler Coming?

There was a huge jolt and the vibration which went through the house sent the biscuit tin rattling across my grandmother's hearth. We were a dozen or so miles away from Glasgow which was taking a pounding but we still felt the vibrations from the explosions, even at that distance. Father had sent us north to Scotland because he felt we would be safer up there just in case Hitler did invade eastern England but on that night, I wasn't so sure. Glasgow was bombed on a regular basis and when the bombing started we would get up in the night and sit there in the darkness drinking tea.

The train that mother, Ian, Marion and I had taken from North Walsham took us on a journey north to Strathaven where my grandmother Susan lived. By the time the Second World War started, she had been a widow for 30 years. Her husband John Paterson had died on 21 October 1909, when father was 12. Grandmother Susan was a big upstanding woman, about six feet tall but very attractive, and was the kind of woman who when she made a decision, the family would know it had been made. She warmly welcomed me into her house, there was no question about that. Families did all they could to help each other; that was in their blood. Although she had been a widow for many years, she was not alone and had a live-in companion, Meg, who was lame. She and granny talked a lot about the countryside and I would listen and I learned from them. I never felt out of place at all because there was the two of them talking to each other and I was part of that.

The farm still had a cowshed and just round the corner from that was the dairy. What I recall was a big table fixed to the wall with a metal dish on it which was used to put the milk in and the cream was skimmed off the top. About two feet from the ceiling was a shelf and that was where grandmother put the cheeses once they were seasoned. My grandfather rarely showed cows when he was alive but he had a reputation for showing cheese and butter, although I do suspect that was perhaps more my grandmother. I used to hear my grandmother talking about showing competitions for butter. Making cheese or butter was a clever way to do business on a dairy farm; if you could not sell the milk then you made it into cheese or butter, and that was also why they survived. There was no Milk Marketing Board back then.

Before long, it was just myself living with my grandmother and Meg. My mother and sister had returned to Norfolk not long after I settled in Strathaven and Ian went to a school in Kilmarnock, which had been moved out of Glasgow because of the war. Scotland and Strathaven were not new to me. I had visited a number of times before on summer holidays or on visits to relatives so I was quite happy and before long started at the local school, Strathaven Academy. School life in Scotland was different from what I had been used to in North Walsham; some of it was better while some of it was not so good. Grandmother lived in a bungalow called Rosemount and there was a playing field between her home and the school, so that turned out to be very convenient for me. I made friends, though some of the boys did not want to be friends with me and a number of them were perpetual fighters. I had not come across that before. I remember some of the teachers well, and the fact that they used the strap up there. If you got something wrong or did something you shouldn't have done you would be called out to the front of the class, made to open your hand and the teacher used the strap. They did not overdo it, I must admit, but when you got the strap it really stung. One of the teachers was particularly strict and I made sure I didn't get the wrong side of him. I enjoyed the arithmetic and geography in Scotland as it was taught well and way ahead of what I had learned in Norfolk but I did feel that the grammar side was not as good. On the whole, I don't think going to Scotland did me any good from a schooling point of view. I stayed up there for the best part of three years and did not come home to Norfolk during that time but father and mother would come up to see us and we were among relations up there.

My wartime evacuation to Scotland was very much a case of me returning to the roots of my family. My mother had been born not far away at Yondercroft on 9 February 1900, and my father had been born at Torfoot, Drumclog, on 24 July 1897. He was educated at Barnock School near Dungavel, and we had lots of friends and relatives in that part of the country. The grandfather I never knew, Mr John Paterson of Torfoot, was very highly respected as one of Avondale's best known and most popular farmers, and there was a great sadness when he died. But the family stretched back way beyond that, with the first known reference to a Paterson being to a William Paterson 'on the last day of May 1660' in the final year of the Commonwealth before Charles II was restored to the throne. Documents talk of a 'sasine' which is the delivery of property, usually land, in Scotland and the early

Marion, Gavin and Ian.

reference comes from the Register of Sasines in Lanarkshire, granting William Paterson land and houses at Huntlawrigg. Soon after, there is reference to Alexander Paterson who inherited farm and land at Hartles and Huntlawrigg before signing a marriage contract with Helen Lindsay. Old documents suggest this is dated 22 December 1692, in the 'reign of our Sovereign Lord and Lady King William and Mary'. There are other references and sasines over the years to the Paterson family and various marriages and land changes but it was with the birth of my grandfather on 24 March 1855, at Rosemount, East Kilbride, that the Paterson family seems to gain real prominence in that part of Scotland. He moved to Torfoot when he was seven and joined the Gilmourton School. Education was an important part of his life and he was influenced very much by one of his teachers, a Mr Thomas Cummins, and apparently spoke often during his life of the influence he had upon him. My grandfather's outlook on life, though I never knew him of course, was of a man who never considered his education complete but instead was forever striving after knowledge as he led his life. He married my grandmother, Susan, who was the youngest daughter of Robert Alston of Newlands, on 15 June 1887, and was elected as a member of the School Board of Avondale in 1888, remaining in that post for the next 21 years until his death, rarely missing a meeting. During that time he worked hard to improve the facilities at his local schools of Gilmourton, Drumclog and Barnock and encourage a more modern approach to teaching. Grandfather ran his farm from an early age and later, when the local farmers formed the Avondale Farmers' Analytical Society, he became heavily involved in that and was ultimately appointed secretary and treasurer, until he became ill in December 1901. Members appreciated his work and presented him with a writing desk and bookcase for his efforts and gave my grandmother a 'beautiful timepiece', according to an account of that period. A loyal churchgoer, he had a deep sense of faith, but one that few truly saw. His close friend, Rev. David A. Rollo, said my grandfather 'never cared to parade his religion, yet deep in his heart there was a true faith in God'. He was superintendent of the Avondale Parish Church at Strathaven for some years too and also helped oversee the construction of Drumclog Memorial Church on Snabe Farm. David Rollo first met my grandfather when he was inducted into the Parish of Avondale in 1893, and gave an insight into my grandfather, suggesting that he could have occupied 'a very influential position among men' had he not chosen and preferred 'the quiet of the country'.

'He was a man of shrewd character, just dealing and fearless courage', wrote Rollo. 'Any cause he took up had his enthusiastic support, and on more than one occasion I had reason to be thankful for his help; most especially in the School Board, where we were fellow members and in the erection of Drumclog Memorial Church.'

Towards the end of the first decade of the twentieth century, his health was failing and he underwent treatment in a Nursing Home in Glasgow. Initially it appeared he was going to get better but he took a turn for the worse and died soon after. His funeral, conducted by Rev. John Muirhead, took place on 23 October 1909 at Avondale Parish Church, where he was a member of the congregation, with a large number of people turning out to pay their last respects to him.

There were so many different aspects to my grandfather and he had talents that not all knew about. It seemed he enjoyed writing poetry. I understand that he even contributed to the 'poet's corner' of the *Hamilton Advertiser* and also turned to his writing when he lost his sons. My grandfather was a clever man, and though he was a farmer he also studied and he had been to university when he was a young man. Although he died at a relatively young age, he achieved a great deal in the 54 years he did live. As well as a dairy farmer, he was an educationalist and he used his university background to help young people better themselves where he could.

My mother was also brought up dairy farming in Ayrshire and that tells a lot about her for a start. When I was at college a few years later I occasionally stayed with the Mitchell family near Kilmarnock at weekends. Everybody in the family would get up in the morning and do the work; that was the standard way a small dairy farm would work. As they were growing up they knew how to do things on the farm and my mother milked for her father; she was paid for it, but that was her upbringing and that was normal procedure on the farm. If you heard two Scots talking about family life, you might hear one say to the other, 'you would go east for a farm and west for a wife'. That was because girls on a farm knew how to do things and my mother was like that and when she came to Worstead she ran the household. If father had taken a small farm, she would probably have been part of the milking gang but he was ambitious with cattle and had a herd of cows on each farm. While she did not do the milking she had the knowledge to do it if necessary. The cookery knowledge of ladies such as mother was first class and when we had guests she would provide all the catering. She knew how to put on a good spread. Father spent his time outside on the farm but she was always there; they were a good team together. They would both work hard but that was how they had grown up.

Mother was born in the house my grandfather built and her father was an Alston – she was Marion Taylor Wright Alston and the Wrights were one of the families that came down from Scotland. They were married on 24 June 1925. Father was keen to make things work and had Uncle James (Alston) as his anchor and his adviser.

At Yondercroft, mother's family home, you could walk from the kitchen straight into the cowshed without having to go out into the farmyard and get wet. Usually, over the cowshed was the 'bothy' and they were rooms for anybody working on the farm. The cows generated heat in the cowshed and that heat would go up and keep the room above warm. Mother, who was often known as May, was a nice looking lady and she was very happy with her life and satisfied with what dad was doing and had no ambition of her own other than to make as good a job as she could for the family; the family was always her first priority.

By the time I turned up in Strathaven, my grandfather – father's father – was long dead, but still remembered, particularly with my grandmother living into old age. I spent the best part of three years with her, but as the war progressed the threat of a German invasion in Norfolk disappeared somewhat as Hitler headed east towards Russia. When it seemed clear to father that the Germans weren't coming to Norfolk I returned home, though Ian stayed in Scotland to complete his education. Things had changed by the time I got back to Norfolk. The home I had left was Manor Farm House, Worstead, but as the war progressed that property was taken over by the Army and mother and father had a choice: either share it with the military or look to live elsewhere. It was this set of circumstances that saw us move to Church Farm, Smallburgh and Holly House, which is still my home today.

The move had much to do with the war and the requirements of the Army, which was looking to defend the Norfolk coastline in a big way. For its headquarters and centre of operations, the Army had set its eyes on the big house on the Worstead Estate, which had been bought by the newspaper tycoon Sir Harold Harmsworth in about 1938. The property was said to have 23 bedrooms and was the estate house

Worstead House, from a print of 1820. Built in the 1790s to a design by James Wyatt, the house was demolished in 1939.

at the time of the sale. It had been built for the Berney Brograve family in the 1790s before it passed to the Rous family in the 1840s. At some stage along the way, the house was added to, though apparently not in a very stylish way. The story goes that Sir Harold had invited his uncle, also named Sir Harold Harmsworth, to stay and he owned another estate near King's Lynn. When he saw the Worstead Estate, the uncle told his nephew the newspaperman 'you've got yourself a nice estate here but you should really do something about that house. It looks like a prison.' So the new owner Sir Harold Harmsworth knocked it down. When the Army finally came to Worstead, expecting to use the big house as their headquarters, they found it was no longer there so they had to look for another, suitable, property. The next biggest house was Manor Farm House in Worstead, our home.

One day, the Army just knocked on the door and told father 'We are taking over this house.' I'm sure that came as a shock to father. The Army said he and mother could still live at Manor Farm if they wanted to but warned them, 'You will need a certificate to get past the sentry and also show it again to park your car in the garage and get in the front door.' So, from then on, he had to show this certificate to get through his own front door and then step over all the bodies of sleeping soldiers to get upstairs. The soldiers were everywhere and used the village hall, which was about 30 yards away from our cowshed, as their NAAFI and built Nissen huts in the Park. In Worstead, the Army had ultimately taken over the village. I wouldn't say there was no ill feeling about it, it was just one of those things that happened when the war came. They set up a training camp and the North Walsham and Dilham Canal was deepened to form a defence against tanks. There were pill boxes and a few gun emplacements as well. Father liked to tell the story about how he went in one day and all the cow shed staff were enjoying a slap-up breakfast, which the soldiers had given them in return for a bucket of milk.

Father had been a tenant farmer all his life but I suppose this was his first nudge towards buying a farm. The situation with the Army in Manor Farm House was far from satisfactory, particularly with mother back at home and us boys eventually coming back home at some stage. When Church Farm, Smallburgh, was for sale there was also another farm which came up at the same time but that was right on the main road, which was fairly busy. Out of the two, Church Farm had the better house. Father favoured it for that reason but also because it was a little quieter and in good order. As it turned out, the other farm sold first so he bought Church Farm and moved in, though he still kept Manor Farm at Worstead as a tenant at that stage. That was his first big move. He had not been that keen on buying but my father and mother were not comfortable in the Manor Farm House under the circumstances. That would have been in 1939; a couple of years or so later – in 1942 – it was where I came home to when I returned from Scotland, midway through the war.

Church Farm, as the name suggests, was opposite Smallburgh Church. The house which went with the farm was known as Holly House and it had an adjoining cottage which was originally the servants' quarters. Just like Manor Farm House at Worstead, Holly House was busy, there were always people calling by and there was a gardener or handyman who did the garden and washed cars or ran messages if necessary.

When father bought the farm he engaged Billy Botwright as his foreman. Billy was a character, he was a horseman and was a good foreman, but he had been in the Army and was a bit rough and ready at times. He had two sons, Wally who lived on the farm and Gordon, who was away in Africa with the Army and eventually got taken prisoner of war and didn't come home until much later on. Billy's wife died

Holly House, Smallburgh.

at some point and by the time I came back from Scotland there was just Billy and Wally in the cottage, which today is part of the house and the farm office. Between them, they helped run the farm.

When we were younger, Wally and I used to shoot together. To kill vermin, most farmers, sooner or later, get hold of a gun. Billy and Wally were both keen on guns, Often, when Wally went ferreting, he stood on one side with the ferrets and I stood on the other side waiting for the rabbits to appear. He put a ferret in the hole and the rabbit would come out at some point and we would shoot it. I would go for long Saturday walks sometimes and shoot a few rabbits or rats; we did need to shoot the rats to keep them down along with the rabbits but we'd sell the rabbits and people would eat them. Once you start shooting vermin it gets into your system on how to handle a gun. I had a 4.10 to start with but with guns you have got to be so careful, you can't go swinging them about. From that we went on to shooting pheasants and partridges. The aim with a shoot is to get the pheasants and partridges flying very high – there is more satisfaction in shooting a high bird, and that is not easy, it is one of the challenges but you always aim to kill the bird outright. It is a country sport and once you have game on the farm and you are good at handling a gun, the two go together. The Withergate Rifle Club has shot on the estate for many years, and still does with our permission, and I was associated with the club for many years. Today, we still have shooting on our land and the gamekeeper, who keeps our vermin under control, puts feeders out to feed the birds regularly.

When we moved to Holly House, we had a lady that came to help keep the house. There was no central heating so we had to put three or more fires in the house in the cold weather. Mostly it was somebody who could do all the jobs and a spot of babysitting if necessary, normally one of the employees' wives who was pleasant and could get on with the jobs without much managing. Some of them were like gold dust as they just kept the whole thing neat and tidy and without any fuss.

At the height of the war, it wasn't just the Army that we were aware of. Coltishall was the big local air base and there were planes going in and out all the time; they were fighters but we had some bombs going off not far away from here. The big danger was from the German bombers, when the fighters attacked them. They just dumped their bombs as they headed for home. We didn't get away from the war completely and there were bombs dropped over Worstead. I remember there was a story, which made the local paper, about a man with a horse in a field with a roller. He was alongside the main road to North Walsham when this German plane dropped some bombs somewhere very close to Worstead. The horse took flight and got away from him. It knew where the gate was and headed straight for it but the roller was too wide to go through the gateposts but the horse broke out of its

Gavin with Withergate Rifle Club.

harness and went off. When the man got back to the farm, the horse was in the stable contentedly eating hay. There was also a tramp who turned up in the village one day. He made a home for himself in one of the straw stacks but everybody was convinced that he was a spy. By the time I came back from Scotland, the real danger from the war had eased, though I did discover that there were a lot of people involved in the war. I later found out that the leader of the Young Farmers' Club in Aylsham and his wife had a secret job reporting on anything suspicious that was going on.

I remember my brother was interested in the Royal Navy when he was at school and he would make models of the big ships. He'd know how many guns they had and how many people were in the crew. I was more interested in the Royal Air Force and if I had to join up that was the way I would have gone. But it didn't happen. We didn't do National Service either as we were both learning about how to run the family farm and how to produce food. That was how farmers contributed to the war effort, by making sure there was enough to eat, and with father it was ensuring there was milk.

The camp which had been built for the Army on the Worstead Estate in 1941 was put to other uses when the war ended. First of all it was used for Prisoners of War and then later, when they all went back home, it was used for displaced persons, people who had lost their homes. When it all fizzled out they either went away or moved into some houses that were built in the area and gradually it was demolished until there was nothing left apart from the pipes underground which we still find now and again. There were people who were not comfortable with the Prisoner of War camp but in those days they did not have much say and if someone made a decision it was going to happen, it happened. The prisoners worked on the land and some of them worked for us and in general they behaved themselves. The only thing we did have happen was that we had some prisoners who were brought in from somewhere else at the time. Gordon, who had been a prisoner, had come home after being repatriated but during his time abroad he had learned to speak German. One day he was working with the PoWs, I think they were loading sheaves of corn at harvest as we were short of labour, and there were two or three of them and they were saying something in German but did not know Gordon spoke German. All of a sudden he exploded and gave them a real dressing down. To this day we still don't know what they were saying and what he said but we do know that he let fly because after that they kept very quiet when he was around.

After my period of education in Scotland, I went to Paston School at North Walsham when I got back to Norfolk. It was a good school, famous as being where Lord Nelson was taught before he went off to sea. Paston School was six miles away from the farm and I would sometimes bike to school but the most convenient, and for me the most enjoyable, way to get to and home from school was to ride a pony. For a lot of those days, I'd ride my pony Peggy to and from school. I used to roll up a small bale of hay and tie it to the saddle and off we would go. There used to be a pub on the corner near the school, it's not there now, but I had an arrangement with the landlord. I'd take my pony and tie her up, put the hay on the hay rack and leave her there all day while I went to school. Once my lessons were over, I'd just saddle her up and off we'd go home again. We'd head off along Yarmouth Road and past the police station with the clatter of hooves sounding out. When the pony

Paston School, North Walsham.

knew she was going home she'd really go. I enjoyed that ride home and if there was a field by the roadside that was clear, we'd head off the road and gallop through the fields. Peggy was a very kind little pony. We had to know about horses because on the farm they were a commodity, but they could be dangerous too, so father thought the quickest way for us to get to know about horses was to buy us a pony each. I did enjoy my pony and would often enter gymkhanas and compete. Ian's pony was called Buttercup but he did not really ride her but I had a friend who was dead keen to ride a pony, so I agreed to start riding the bigger pony, Buttercup, and he rode the little one, Peggy. Buttercup was an appaloosa, with broken colour; she was a half thoroughbred and had a bit of spirit. Buttercup was fiery and she could ride a person up on her back sometimes and I have known her to get tricky and throw people off. There was one day on the farm when an old friend of the family

43

came to see us. He was a horse person and asked if Buttercup was still about. I said she was in the paddock and he asked if he could take her for a ride as he had ridden her in the past but I warned him that if he was going to take her up the field he had to take care. I knew that when she got to the bottom hedge, she would come back at a gallop because that is what I did with her. I watched her start from behind the pit and then saw her coming back at a gallop and I knew as she got close to the hedge she probably would not stop but would go over it. She got within about 20 yards of it, put the brakes on and stuck her feet in the ground. He went up right over her head and came down with a thump. He was a middle-aged man by that time and I went forward to him fearing the worst. I said, 'Are you all right?' He didn't seem all that ruffled, said he was all right and commented that the old mare 'has still got some go in her'. She was temperamental and if she got upset it would not be pretty, you just had to go with her. I used to take her to gymkhanas and there was a girl I knew at them who could handle a horse. She would jump Buttercup and she'd usually win on her.

When I wasn't going to school on the pony, I'd bike there. Some days, father would be in North Walsham for a meeting so I'd wait for him to finish and stick the bike on the back of the car and we'd come home together. I quite enjoyed my time at Paston School but I have to say that by that time I was more interested in the farm than my schoolwork. We did jobs on the farm and learned from the men. We perhaps got a little pocket money. Thinking about it, we must have done because we always seemed to have enough money to buy sweets. There was always a bit of contention about how quickly they were eaten. Some people ate them within two days while others hung on to their monthly sweet ration for a while longer. By that stage, I was so interested in the farm and what was going on that there was not too much danger of me ever becoming a scholar. At the end of the school day I just wanted to get back home to the farm. I played some sport at school, I did a bit of everything such as football and hockey and even cricket, though that was never my game having been knocked out that day with a cricket ball. I did also join the Army Cadet Force at school and I remember one day we were all on the playing field waiting for someone from the Army to come and inspect us. It was a hot day and some of the boys even fainted while we waited because the man from the Army was late turning up.

I did the exams I was required to do but can't really remember how well I did and I eventually left school at 17, which was earlier than I might otherwise have done but father knew I was ready to come home and start work. Both my brother and I became the extra labour that would be available when there was some cattle work to be done. The plan was that we went into the cowshed to learn from the herdsman and to understand the work, and that is exactly what we did. That was our first jobs.

The farm operation had grown by the time Ian and I were leaving school. In the years before, during and after the war, father expanded the farming side of things considerably. At the same time as buying and moving to Church Farm, Smallburgh, he hired Bunn's Farm at Worstead which was of 246 acres and run with Manor Farm. At the same time he gave up Crostwight Hall Farm on the understanding that his brother-in-law Rob Alston was to take it on, which he did for many years.

Church Farm soon became father's main interest and it was here that he built his first completely new cowshed for 72 cows. When the time came for entry on 11 October 1939, just a month after the war had started, father bought 58 Ayrshire heifers from Hendry Bros for £30 each, purchased on the telephone. He told me later, 'I did not see them till they arrived at North Walsham station and a very useful lot they were. Prices rose from then on and some were sold after several years milking at double what they cost.' Father continued to build and expand and when he bought Dilham Hall from Mr W. Faulkes in 1943 he put up another brand new shed for 72 cows. It was 277 acres and Mr Faulkes had farmed it all his life. He was a traditional horseman and when he sold it to father, he was very specific in saying that he did not want father as the new owner to bring tractors on to this farm. Mr Faulkes still lived in the house – that was part of the deal – so he would see if father did take a tractor on to that farm. The arrangement over no tractors did last for a little while until father said that with everything going in the direction of tractors and mechanisation, he couldn't oblige Mr Faulkes any longer and he then began to use tractors at Dilham Hall.

All of these farming transactions that father was conducting brought with them changes in the way we farmed. It meant that we were getting more tractors and reducing our reliance on horses. As the tractors came along, there were also changes in the landscape as we took out a number of hedges to make for better cultivation and one-way ploughing which helped because it meant there were no furrows or other impediments to cross. All the land was run as four units and between the operations it wasn't long before we had quite a fleet of vehicles and machinery: five combine harvesters with dressing machines and each farm having a lorry to take the milk to Norwich Co-op Dairy. Those lorries were also used to take cattle to market and sugar beet to the Cantley factory.

We were one of the first farms in the area to get the Massey Ferguson combine harvester. 'Bubbles' drove it – that was Gordon the soldier and brother of Wally. They would work together, with Wally sacking the corn. On those early combines there was no container for the corn to go into, it just went into a corn sack and had to be tied up and then slid down on a slide to the ground and had to be picked up later to be carted to the shed. Each bag weighed 18 stones, so you can imagine that was hard

James Paterson with his first combine harvester.

work. Often the herdsman, to get some overtime, would go back in the lorry and pick the sacks up at the end of the day. When later you had a container on the combines, the corn was augured straight into the trailer and that made a big difference.

There were always trains going by the farm in my younger days, and of course they were all steam engines. We would have gone by steam train to Scotland from North Walsham when I left home during the war to stay with my grandmother. The railway would go from Norwich to Wroxham and then North Walsham and when the railway went past Worstead it was uphill which meant the engines had to puff hard. 'Puff, puff, puff' they used to go and blow cinders out as they went. Unfortunately, that could set fire to the crops, which they did one day. In that crop was one of those early combines we were trying to reap with. The cinders from the steam train dropped on the straw, which was very quickly put to fire. When the driver saw the fire he thought he would have plenty of time to get to the gate but there was a breeze coming across the field and the fire spread that fast that it blocked his access to the gate. Our man on the combine got the breeze up so he headed for the hedge and the bank and went over it in the combine into the next field. If he hadn't done that, we would have lost the combine as well.

'Puff, puff' was a dangerous caper in those days and a big risk for burning crops but the engine driver would have no idea that he had set the field on fire as he would have been long gone. It would have been before the war when that happened.

I was only a young lad of about six or seven but remember it well because the field was just on the outside of the village and the fire could so easily have spread to the houses as they were not far away. Trains setting fire to crops was not uncommon but we only had that happen once to us.

I was always out on the farm, often with father or with one of the other men. I got to know the men very well and a lot of them were special to us. When I left school that is when I started to do more things, moving from the boy's jobs to the men's jobs. Father's idea was if you learn to do the work before taking on the management you are then in a position to explain how it should be done; it was just something we grew into. But soon, I had to gain some more formal training for my life ahead on the farm, and once again that saw me return to Scotland.

I must have been 19 when I went to Glasgow Agricultural College. My digs were just off the north end of Sauchiehall Street. They were comfortable and convenient for where I wanted to be. We would walk out to Sauchiehall Street and catch the bus or tram, which went down about two thirds of the way, and then walk up Blythwood Square. A bit further along was the college where we went to seminars and meetings, looking at the various angles of farming. I went up to college with two friends; Hugh Fleming was a friend through family connections and lived in Sussex and the other was Matthew Mitchell whom I knew from the Aylsham Young Farmers' Club. Hugh was a character and we had a great time at college. Matthew and I stayed in digs and I think Hugh stayed with some relatives up there for what was a six-month farming course.

The daily lectures were about all aspects of farming. I got to know one of the lecturers quite well and every so often he would say to me 'Is that what you do in Norfolk?' When it came to arable farming, wheat and sugar beet, we found the wheat system was slightly different between Scotland and Norfolk. The lecturer would say you do not stack wheat when it is wet but that is a crop you can get away with stacking if it is slightly wet, because of the condition of the sheaves. At such a point he would look at me and say 'Is that what happens in Norfolk?', inviting me to contradict it if I wanted to. Glasgow was a pure and simple lecture room; for the practical session we went to Auchencrow in Ayrshire, where we went to look at cows. As a cow man, father's opinion was that I would learn more about cows in Scotland than anywhere else. We would take the bus from Glasgow for the day and it would drop us at the farm where we would learn more about cows. To some extent I was a little disappointed we didn't spend more time in Auchencrow, as that was not only more hands-on experience for us of studying the cows but was also near father's old home in Scotland, which was only about three miles away.

Most weekends I would head out of Glasgow on the bus to Strathaven to visit relatives. I had an uncle and aunt who lived in Strathaven, though my grandmother Susan, whom I stayed with during the war, was dead by then. Sometimes Hugh Fleming came to Strathaven as well. We also went to the Mitchells and there was a very practical dairy farming lesson to be learned there from my point of view. In fact, it was an education in what life was like on small farms in Scotland, and perhaps a lesson my parents were keen for me to learn. The Mitchells had three daughters and a son, who was the youngest. On a morning, the family all got up together, including visitors who blundered about and did not help too much. When the first daughter and the mother got up, their job was to make breakfast and the beds; the other daughter and the father milked the cows; and the third daughter took the little brother to feed the calves. This was a small dairy farm with stock on it, with all the work done by the time it was breakfast. After that the girls went off to work, they were 18 or so, and the father would go out to plough or do whatever had to be done on the farm. The process was probably repeated in the afternoon, but the important thing is that it was done by the family, so as they grew up they understood how to do jobs on the farm because the oldest took it on to learn to do a job and they would take a young one with them. That is an education bar none in my opinion and growing up doing the job is what my father did. That is how he gained knowledge of cows, chickens and pigs. Perhaps you can get such knowledge by sitting and listening to someone teaching you what to do, but it is not the same as actually doing the job, especially if things are going wrong. That is when you really learn, especially with cows, calves and chickens. I had already done most of it but I was getting a glimpse of what father did, watching as he grew up when he was young. He did not go to college for any length of time but knew that doing the job is what really teaches you about farming.

I was only in Glasgow for six months, right enough, and during the week I don't recall we did much socialising, perhaps went to the pictures occasionally. If you stuck to the routine in the B&B, which we probably did, you were fed for breakfast, you got your lunch at college, and we were there for mealtimes in the evening. The social side was at weekends when we went to those relations and they were pleased to see us with plenty to chat about. I cannot really remember doing much in Glasgow itself. There are bits of Glasgow that are very interesting and there are bits of Glasgow that you would rather not know about. By the time I came back from Glasgow, my knowledge of farming was taking shape nicely. I had been to college, I had spent my whole life on the farm, watching the men, listening to the conversations of father's friends and enthusiastically taking it all in. All I wanted to do was to get to work on my own farm, and for me that couldn't happen soon enough.

Chapter Four

A Young Farmer

Ted had never seen a Scottish kilt before, let alone worn one. But when he saw a photograph of father in full Scottish evening dress with his kilt and plaid, the young black American farmer who was staying with us was intrigued. Spotting Ted's interest, mother asked if he would like to see it on, and then seizing the moment invited him to pose in it. Well, he laughed at the idea but he was game and got dressed up in the kilt. He roared with laughter when he saw it on; so did Ed, another young American visitor. They had been invited over to England when I was a member of Aylsham Young Farmers' Club and were staying with us. It must have been the early 1950s and the pair of them were in the American equivalent which was known as 4H. The county club had organised a dance in the Norwood Rooms in Norwich, where the dress code was formal evening dress, and they were our honoured guests.

'Would you like to wear the kilt to the dance, Ted?' mother asked.

'I could not possibly do that ma'am,' he politely replied but mother persisted and urged him to at least wear the waistcoat that went with it for the occasion, and this he did. It was father's waistcoat but Ted liked the idea and so he wore it very proudly to the dance and kept showing people. In fact, I believe he even took the waistcoat back to America with him.

Ed and Ted had been picked, or were volunteers, to take up a visit to Europe which included the UK and Norfolk. When Ed and Ted came over they were welcomed by the National Young Farmers in this country and then found themselves in Norfolk where we had the chance to host them. The idea was they would see how everything in farming worked here. We had the space at Church Farm, so we took them in and they both stayed in our guest room at Holly House, which was the best room in the house with an en suite shower. It must have been the first morning after they arrived that Ed came down and said something that struck me later.

'If my parents knew I was sleeping in the same room as a black man,' he said, 'they would have me comin' back home straight away. They would not expect it.'

We hadn't really thought about it but Ed, who was white, and Ted, who was a young black farmer, travelling together and sharing a room would have been considered extremely out of the ordinary in America at the time. But they were quite happy together, they did not complain and nothing else was said on the subject after that. And it certainly made no difference to us. From there we took them round various farms and to other events, possibly the Royal Norfolk Show, and the whole thing went perfectly well and their different backgrounds did not make any difference to us, or them. They got on very well together and indicated that they were quite happy to do what they were asked to do.

This was just one of the many adventures and opportunities that the Aylsham Young Farmers' Club presented to me and I was anxious to make the most of every opportunity offered, that was the spirit of our club and I enjoyed every minute of my membership. It should also be said that I learned a huge amount too, not just about farming but about life in general and about social skills, and made many, many friends in Norfolk and far beyond.

Young Farmers' Clubs usually started when a farmer or farming families in a district were looking for somewhere for their children to go as they got into their mid-teens to make friends and learn in a fun way. There was still petrol rationing, so we had some restrictions on getting around as you weren't meant to use up your petrol for enjoyment purposes but that didn't stop us.

While the nearest club to us at the time was at Stalham, we'd also heard about Aylsham Young Farmers' Club through a friend of my father's. Several of his acquaintances, mostly the Scottish farmers, had family going there and they had helped start it, so that's the club we joined. The club was of a good standard and we met in the St John Ambulance rooms on a Tuesday once a week, except in the heat of the summer when most of us were tied up all hours with the harvest. The meetings began at 7.30pm, but we'd normally get there at about 7.15pm and settle down. There was a committee of seven or eight, a club leader who was usually a senior member, and the chairman, secretary and treasurer who were usually the eldest of the young farmers. They set the pattern for the club. There was a farmer who was older who put forward ideas but it was the committee which ran the club. There was usually a broad menu of discussion and activities on the programme at the meeting; the idea was to try to keep it interesting to as many people as possible. We would have a speaker who came to talk about a farming subject and we also used to visit farms and do stock judging. There was often an element of competition within the programme. There would be about 25 of us at each meeting and it was a 50/50 male/female split. We were mostly from farming families and had been encouraged by our parents to join Young Farmers' Clubs to learn more about farming and we all did the various roles, though if there was any catering to be done the girls usually did that.

For us, Young Farmers' covered all aspects of life and was a chance to learn but with no drastic effect if we got it wrong; that was the beauty of it. It was about getting experience of things that we might need, or want, to do when we grew up but without any repercussions, but it was also about having fun.

You had to be 15–26 to be a member. I was about 17 when I joined, Ian was already a member and we had a cousin – Gavin Alston from Sco Ruston (who, like me, was named after my mother's father) – who also went along. He had a business of his own hatching chickens over and above his father's business. There was a huge amount of chicken hatching going on – he was hatching hundreds at a time and he sold them on the open market. We used to pick him up, or go with him, with the three of us in the same van going to the same place. We all had vans then; they were useful around the farm as you could cart anything in them, they were just a handy vehicle to have. Ours was red, like a Post Office van. Gavin used his van to deliver his chicks in. We could rough it in those days and we would make ourselves comfortable sat on a box in the back as he drove us to the club.

The social side was very important; we always had an annual dance and we

Aylsham Young Farmers' Club.

51

always wanted to attract members of other Young Farmers' Clubs along as well. There were several clubs that we were friendly with, Wymondham in particular. We played football and hockey matches and somebody was in charge of getting teams together and quite often we were asked to get a team up for things that we didn't know much about. Hockey was the most popular because the girls could play as well and if you had played the game at school you were usually okay but otherwise it wouldn't be so easy. I played football at school but got used to hockey and enjoyed it. I soon discovered that no-one wanted to play left wing so if I offered to play in that position I could usually get a game. We played other clubs like Diss or Wymondham and if there was a barrel of beer at stake the games were usually a bit more active.

The club was all very grown up and properly run; we would hold our AGM and learned to take part in the organisation of the club and activities and also how to speak in public. Everyone was encouraged to take part. We had debates and our club had the approach that we would always take part in everything the county put on. They had competitions for public speaking or stock judging and a whole range of other things. I remember one of the funny things that happened was when we had a competition among the boys for darning a sock. At the time I was one of the people who were pushing for things to be done and I said 'Someone has got to enter.' Sure enough, someone said 'Why don't you do it?' So I did, and it turned out I won but I had watched my mother darning socks quite a lot so I knew roughly how it would go. One of the most valuable assets any club could have was some nice looking girls because that attracted other clubs to come along to our dances, and as I remember Aylsham did have its fair share of pretty girls.

The longer it went on with the club the more I felt that I was enjoying having fun with young people and learning at the same time. And that was fantastic. I think the Young Farmers' Club helped bring a lot of young people out of their shells because we were doing all sorts of things and it did not matter if something went wrong, the idea was to give it a try and see what you could do. A lot of the people I know in farming were those I knew from Young Farmers days and I would often meet them all over the place over the years and they all say the same thing: 'What a wonderful thing the Young Farmers' organisation was at that time.'

I learned so much; I learned to get up on my feet and put a sentence together that made sense, I hope. If you lost your temper in a debate you did not get marks for that; we were taught to speak correctly in public without losing our tempers and, most importantly, taught to listen to people as well. I have never been great at public speaking but equally I was not afraid to get up and say what I thought. At Young Farmers you could take part in events that the clubs organised and there were no grown-ups looking down their noses at you thinking what a silly boy you were. It was all fun.

As time passed I began to play a greater role in the running of the club and later started to have a role at county level too. I was an enthusiastic member and very proud to be part of Aylsham Young Farmers' Club. This eventually led to a place on the committee for me. Every two or three years someone would propose you for the committee, often to do something in particular, and this happened for the girls as well. If they were trained as a secretary they would always get a job! Everybody found their niche and the opportunity to use their ability to help run the clubs. You became very proud of your club and the ability of your club to take part in everything. I think we were led very, very well by members. Father would hear about how the club was doing and we invited parents to various things and it became very much a farming family affair. My sister Marion also joined.

Eventually, I was surprised to be elected chairman of Aylsham Young Farmers' Club. The club leader at the time said to me soon after, 'I'm sorry I was not able to attend the meeting where the chairman was elected. Can you tell me who it was?' I told him it was me, to which he said 'You'll be all right but don't forget you have to win the NFU trophy.' I think he was throwing down a challenge to me. The NFU Trophy was won by the club which had the most points from the events held throughout the year and we had won it for the previous two years. As it turned out, we did win the NFU trophy that year I was chairman – for the third year in a row – and probably the fourth year in a row after that as well. But that was special and every club took part and tried to do the best it could to win that award.

Each club had two members on the county committee. At Aylsham it was myself and our club secretary, Josephine Duffield, who was also a Miss Norfolk Young Farmer in her day. We went to the meeting to choose the next county chairman and vice chairman and on this occasion we had all generally agreed who should be the next vice chairman of the county and it was my friend David Richardson from Wymondham. He was the preferred choice to go forward to be vice chairman and then go on to be chairman. We had spoken about it and he had not said much and when we got there on the day for the meeting he was proposed and seconded. But he took us all by surprise when he stood up and said 'I am sorry I cannot do it as I am getting married.'

'I do not see that stops you being vice chairman,' I replied to which he said 'but I think that stops me,' which we all laughed about. We had been so sure he was going to be the man for the job that it left us wondering what to do, including Lady Upshaw, who was our president and she was fantastic, a wonderful president. There was a deadly hush and mumbling around the room and we were not getting

Lady Upshaw with the author (right).

anywhere. Josephine looked across at me and mouthed 'Why don't you do it?'

'I'm too old, I am 25' I said to her, but I must have spoken a little too loudly as someone in the room pointed out I wasn't 26, so was still eligible. So I took it on and that is how I got to be vice chairman of Norfolk Young Farmers.

That would have been in 1955 when I became vice chairman, with John Garner as the chairman. John was a good chairman and good to follow. I was a little flummoxed about not having time to think about it but somebody had to stand up and be counted and I could think of no reason not to. We had tried to avoid people saying 'no' when they were proposed for something so I could not back out. I took the job on and started going to meetings and took a strong interest. It was good experience to be vice chairman before taking on the chairman's job but things were about to take quite a serious turn as regards the affairs of Norfolk's Young Farmers. The county organiser was paid for by the county education department. It was an appointment that if it didn't work out, it was difficult to get rid of the person in the role that easily. We had just acquired a new county organiser and it soon emerged that he was not what we had anticipated. In short, we were not at all comfortable with our new organiser. It was a tricky situation but thankfully Lady Upshaw took us through that and the organiser soon left. It was not a pleasant situation but being part of it was one of those experiences that stood me in good stead, the sort of experience you would not want to go through too often but it was good to be guided through it by someone like Lady Upshaw. So, the organiser just disappeared and thankfully was not heard of again. It did, however, leave me with an extra little job to do. The county organiser had traditionally written notes for the *Eastern Daily Press*, which appeared in the newspaper once a week on a Friday. John Garner did it for six months and I took it over from there. The idea was to write in the EDP about what the county committee was doing, advertise events and keep members in touch with the county committee.

Eventually, I became county chairman. I decided to really throw myself into the role and be a very active chairman. What I decided I would do was to get the programme from each Young Farmers' Club in Norfolk and that I would call on each club in the county once in the summer and once in the winter to show my nose, tell them about the county's plans and activities and to listen to what they had got to say. There were 22 clubs in the county at the time, so it was a significant commitment on my part. As a result, I did not go to my own club as much as I had done in the past but I became more involved with what was going on at county level and enjoyed getting around each club very much. Funnily enough, that led to other things.

One of the last meetings I went to during my term of office was at Downham Market. I obtained the programme to see what that club was doing at its meetings and whether any of the events were of interest to me. It transpired that Downham Market had arranged a meeting where a chap who had applied for a Nuffield Scholarship was their guest speaker. It was his subject which had attracted my attention: 'the relationship between the farmer, the farmer's wife, the herdsman's wife and the herdsman'. I thought this was a peculiar thing to be doing a study into but he had done the work and was now speaking about it. I did think that when I went to that meeting at Downham Market I was probably the person most interested in his talk in the room at that time. At the end of his speech we got chatting and I asked him how he came to get the Nuffield Scholarship. He said he had this idea and filled in an application form and was then invited for an interview and it went from there. He had some forms in his case and he gave one to me. It also coincided with quite a difficult time in my life. Father had been ill, seriously ill, and Ian and I were playing a bigger part in running the farms to the extent that I was doing little else but work apart Young Farmers' on a Tuesday night and maybe having a meal out with friends on a Saturday. Father, thankfully, was a little better and I had also decided in my own mind that if an opportunity presented itself, I would go for it. That led to me attending the Downham Market meeting, getting talking to this chap and taking the Nuffield Scholarship papers he gave me. I was not sure whether I'd fill them in or not but as the opportunity knocked I suppose I talked to Dad about it and he felt the same way and saw that I had been tied up with the farm and not done much else. So I filled the papers in with two references, one from the bank manager and the other from Mr Charles Wharton, a well-known farmer and character from Acle district. Not bad I thought, a bank manager and well-known farmer, so I sent them in, probably thinking I'd get nothing back but before long I received an invitation to attend an interview.

What I wanted to study was grassland management and dairy farming in Australia and New Zealand, and going to those places was the key for me. However, I was to be disappointed. I got a letter back to say that unfortunately there had been a lot of people asking for Australia and New Zealand and that I could not go but they would like to offer me an alternative because my application warranted it. They asked would I like to go to Holland, Denmark, Sweden and Finland, which was actually completely the opposite of what I wanted, and I knew I should not see what I really wanted to see in those countries but thought that maybe I should take it anyway. If nothing else, the timing was right; I could go now but would not be able to go at a later date. I was disappointed but decided to give it a go and see what I could see.

Oddly enough, a Saturday night or two before I went to that meeting at Downham Market I was having a meal somewhere in Yarmouth with friends and we ended up on the pier where there was a hand reader. There were three or four of us and we all thought that we would get our palms read. The gipsy palm reader was looking at my hand for a bit and then said that I will live for a long while yet and that she also saw me travelling abroad soon. It went through my mind that I could not see me travelling at that point. I came out of that place and said 'That won't be going to happen' but then this trip cropped up, so I did travel abroad at that time.

I had a little MG sports car which I put on the boat and sailed over to Holland. It was the summer of 1957 when I set off courtesy of the Nuffield Scholarship on a journey that would take me to Holland, Denmark, Sweden and Finland. Someone else had planned my trip and then given me a list of people to meet, booking me into hotels and arranging a set of meetings to go to every day to see different things. In Holland, I spent three or four days somewhere close to Amsterdam and went to the local office of the pedigree Friesian society. It was mainly the cow side I was seeing and how they integrated the breeding side as well. I must admit, I was thinking 'What have I let myself in for?' but at least I did not have much to worry about as I had been told where I should go and I had instructions about how to do it. I did, however, make one mistake when driving in Holland. I had to go back on the road at one stage and when I stopped and turned round I went on the wrong side of the road to where I should have been driving and met a car coming the other way, with the driver waving his arms furiously, telling me I was on the wrong side of the road.

From Holland I made my way in the MG through Germany and across to Denmark where I had two calls, one at Copenhagen and the other on the small island of Funen. In Denmark I stayed on an estate not unlike the Worstead Estate and that was of interest as I needed to see what they were doing and how they were doing it. I stayed with the estate manager and lived with him, which made a whole difference because I got the feel of the estate and the family and what they were doing and I did enjoy that. As it turned out, one of his jobs at that time was inspecting his estate cottages, which was not unlike Worstead again and proved very useful for me with our cottages. He took me out and told me how he did it and that was quite educational for me with the similarities to Worstead, especially as it had woodland as well. I really meant to go back and see that family but never got round to it.

In Sweden, I was shown farming methods and from there I drove on into Finland. I certainly covered some miles in my MG because I went to a place called Oulu which is right at the top of the country in an area of the midnight sun. I have a photograph of the clock tower at midnight where you can see both hands over each other and that was taken in daylight. The man turned out to be the field officer of the Ayrshire Society in Finland and I met him again when he came to England with the Ayrshire Society of Finland sometime after that to see my brother who kept Ayrshires. He was good fun and I enjoyed the trip but he said to me 'You are not saying very much.'

'Well, I am taking it all in,' I assured him. I could not say to him that there was not too much to see but he told me I was being very polite and that the last chap who visited was so damned rude he had to tell him to shut up. He took me on the farm where there was a dairy unit and there were two machines for milking – we had six at that point and had as many as 16 later on. I did perhaps understand what the other 'rude' chap was saying but unlike me, he had obviously spoken his mind. Finland had a parlour system with two machines, though we were still milking in the cowshed, but had six machines so they were less advanced than we were. We were probably one of the last to do away with the cowshed because father liked it.

I had to say I was very disappointed when I got the reply from Nuffield and the trip to Scandinavia was not nearly as good as if I had gone to Australia and New Zealand, however you take what you are offered and get on and do it. Part of the arrangement if you took one of the trips was that you had to be prepared to speak at farmers meetings and therefore I had to make notes. The way I did that was to write a letter every two days and send it home to England. There was some personal stuff in it to my parents but the male secretary we had at the time would type it up so that when I got home it was all typed up which I thought was a good move. The only snag was that I had three times as much information as I needed for the report I had to present to the Nuffield Trust. But I did also give some talks as well. Some things I found interesting, some of it was very good, some not so good. As the man in Finland said, I was keeping very quiet and not saying to him that 'in England we are way ahead of what you are doing'. That must have been what the other chap had told him before me. What I was hoping to see was a streamlined herd in Australia and New Zealand and how they managed that. I have been to Australia since, though that was more for a holiday. However, I did meet a lot of nice people on the trip to Scandinavia and it was a different experience for me. It also showed me examples of what not to do. The whole set up was quite exciting and sometimes you learn what not to do as much as what you should do but I liked the people in Denmark very much, they were super and the trip to Finland was a bit different where the farmers were also foresters and when they ran out of work in the winter they, like us, had forestry to look after. At the end of my trip, my friend Willie Alston flew to Finland to meet me and we drove back to England together in the MG.

But this all came out of Young Farmers and was one of the many opportunities that it brought my way. After my term of office as county chairman ended, I faded out of Young Farmers and left it in the safe hands of a new generation of enthusiastic young people. I did enjoy Young Farmers; I think it was a wonderful organisation at the time but in the end it was what you made of it. I cannot speak highly enough of the Young Farmers because it gave us opportunities to do things and go to places. It was a good club and there were always opportunities to learn and there were a lot of parents that supported us with advice and helping with arrangements and that was marvellous. That was all part of our lives as we grew older but I think it was so important. You would always have a go at something; even if you thought you could not do it, you had a go and found that you were much better at it than you thought and that was a good lesson to learn. That was the whole spirit of the club and why it was so very good for us.

I met some people I never, ever expected to meet. That resulted in some interesting house guests, not only a young black American in the 1950s, but a former German soldier staying with us and so soon after the end of World War Two! This was before I went to Scandinavia and I was in my early 20s. He had been in the German Army and wasn't sure what he would do with himself when the war ended but had an idea that he would live in the countryside. He was about 25 and had decided he was looking specifically for a farmer with one daughter. As it turned out, he found that farmer and married his only daughter and started to farm the land but naturally wanted to learn more about farming methods. That is how he came to England. He ended up in Norfolk and we agreed to look after him during his stay. Everything was fine – I don't recall any problems when he stayed with us – and in exchange I went to Germany. He took me to farms and we also went on a trip up the Rhine as the farm was not too far from the river. The main thing I can remember about that is being told the story of Lorelei, a girl who would stand on a rock with not too many clothes on and sing out over the river, distracting the people on the boats who would run aground on the rocks and then the locals would pick up the debris. I did also note that they were running tractors on different fuel to us. They built frames between the back and front wheels and put a cylinder on it to carry the gas or fuel, which apparently came from making schnapps out of potatoes. I had never seen that before. Language was a problem as I could not speak German, though he spoke quite good English. Even though the war had only ended a few years before, the fighting was not mentioned on either side.

Ed and Ted weren't our only American guests. There were two others who came to stay with us, Larry Royer from Illinois and Joe Fore from California. They came to Norfolk for a fortnight and stayed with a couple of families including a few days at Holly House. During that time Larry and Joe travelled around this part of Norfolk looking at various farms. They had a good time, saw a lot of things and were well entertained. We knew they had enjoyed themselves because soon after they left a letter arrived at Holly House. They must have written and posted it before they left. They thanked us for the good time they had and invited myself and my friend Dick Seaman to go over to America and see them. As it happened, Dick was not able to go so I invited Willie Alston to go with me instead. We initially headed to Canada on our way to Illinois, mainly to see some Canadian airmen we knew who had been based in Norfolk during the war.

We'd become friends with the Canadian RAF fellows through horses. When they were based in Norfolk, they had been keen to meet people who had a pony or horse for them to ride because that was what they were used to doing back home. We knew them well and this trip to America gave us the chance to go and call in on them as it was more or less on the route. So we decided to drop by. The war was like that and you stayed in touch with people and if you had a chance to see them again, you did. How we got to know them so well was that my uncle Rob Alston had a horse that he could not handle so he invited them to break it in. It was a frightening horse to ride but they took it over and got it broken in. It was ingrained into them to break horses in. So, we arranged to meet them in Canada on our way to Illinois. As it turned out, we only saw one of the airmen we knew but it was good to drop by.

From Canada, we went over to Illinois to Larry's. His father worked for the local council but also had a small piece of land that he cultivated. He grew crops and kept a few pigs which they fed on the scraps from the house. Larry had a plan that along with his friend, Willie and I would drive across to California and he would bring us back as well. But his mother had other ideas and told him: 'Larry, you know you have got work to do before you do anything like that.'

I asked Larry what the work was and it turned out to be hoeing crops in a small field of about two acres. I said if you get two more hoes, Willie and I will help you do it. We were used to handling tools so that is what we did. Larry was happy, his mother was happy, but she was determined he was not going to take off and leave some work for his father. With the work done we drove to California, but it was a tough trip. We were there and back within a week on a journey that would normally take a week to get across there by car and another week to get back.

We all took it in turns to drive Larry's car and drove continuously which did mean that to some extent we didn't see as much of the country as would have liked. The part I remember was going over the Rocky Mountains, that was dramatic and the roads were good; we would get up to 70 or 80mph quite easily without any worries about going too fast, though Larry did like to go at 90mph with just one finger on the steering wheel. I didn't like that too much, I got edgy when he did it. He was a funny lad, quite excitable in many ways. Larry had a personal trick and liked to walk into a room and start to 'sell' whatever was in front of him and he was funny at it. Along the way, we stopped at one place supposedly for something to eat in a restaurant but Larry went forward to the bar till and immediately said 'Hhow much am I bid for this?' and he started to sell it. He was funny and did it well and before long he had everybody in the place laughing. We had a round of drinks but eventually we decided to get some food. Larry was still in the thick of it 'selling' the till and by that time the people at the bar were enjoying themselves. They were saying to Larry 'Go on, sell it again,' which he did and they were buying him drinks each time and I could see he was going to be as tiddly as a tot. We went through to the restaurant and had something to eat and left him to it. When we came back, he was still going at it and the whole place was roaring with laughter but we were ready to get back on the road. As we left the bar, Larry turned round and said that he would drive.

'If you are going to drive, then I am going to walk,' I told him. He was dumbfounded but Willie backed me up. When we got back in the car I kept the keys and drove. Larry jumped in the back in a huff and went to sleep. When we stopped again sometime later, his attitude was a little different.

'None of my friends would have stood up to me like that,' Larry said, 'but you were probably right.'

'I hadn't come all this way to end up in a car smash,' I said, and we were fine after that.

We went past the massive rock carvings at Mount Rushmore, sleeping in the car and driving all the time and eventually we arrived in California but there was soon more drama. Everything was arranged, people were expecting us and Joe announced he was taking us out for a slap-up steak meal.

'I can tell you, it is the best steak in this part of the world,' he announced.

We arrived at a restaurant where Joe introduced us as two Englishmen from Norfolk in England. At that, the man turned round and said he was not entertaining two Englishmen.

'I fell out with too many of them when I was over in England.'

We never found out what was behind that but Joe took control, grabbed him by the elbow told him how we had entertained him in England and then took him out the back. When they came back, the man said, 'I'm sorry, I was very rude, what happened with me in England is nothing to do with you.' We got over that better than I thought we would because the man had not expected to be meeting Englishmen. But the meat was absolutely fantastic. We had a big oval plate and the steak was overlapping both ends of it and I thought I would not eat all of that but it was like ice cream, the meat just melted in my mouth. It was good, so good it was the best steak I ever ate in my life, a remarkable piece of meat. We paid for that and left.

When we reached the west coast we realised that California is not the wettest place in the world to be farming and irrigation was one of the major areas we looked at and how the Americans had created channels to feed the water through. To some extent we are doing the same thing now on our land in Norfolk with our own irrigation project. It was an interesting trip, but also frustrating because despite how far we had travelled we didn't see much of the country but we did call at the Grand Canyon on the way back and stopped at the top for something to eat before we drove on. We had been all the way to California, stayed for two days, and then drove back within a week so we did not waste any time. When we got back to Illinois, we took in some agricultural shows and then left Larry to get on with his work. He was an excitable character, and in the years after I left, I always wondered what happened to him. A few years later, I had the chance to find out. I knew a police officer from Norfolk who was going over to America on an exchange visit, and it turned out that he was going to Illinois. I told him I knew someone in Illinois and the story about Larry and where he lived. I said I would just like to know how he was now as he was a bit harum-scarum back then. I knew he would either be locked up or be very successful and doing well. I asked the policemen if he had any way of discreetly inquiring with the local US police about whether Larry has settled down with a family and that I would be very interested to know the answer. When he got back to England the officer sent me a note to say he had found a man with a similar name to Larry's and that he had made a few inquiries and that he seemed to be working hard on something to do with the local council and that he was very successful, was settled down, married and had a family. I was pleased to know that he did have his head screwed on after all.

What Young Farmers did was to give us experience and friendship and many of us missed that once we had left the organisation. You could join in your teens and you'd get more and more involved with the club as you got into your 20s and then when you were 26 you are no longer a member as you are too old. It was such a big part of our lives and then suddenly there was nothing for us to do on the social side of farming any more. There was an occasion when I was talking to a friend, David Richardson, and we began to talk about how we were missing meeting up with people like we did at Young Farmers.

'It's such a pity we can't still get together and meet up like we used to when we were members,' I said, 'a pity there is not another organisation we could go to.' It wasn't long before we were thinking along the same lines of 'Why don't we set one up so we could keep in touch with each other?' We got a list of people together that we thought might be interested and eventually looked at forming an 'after Young Farmers' club that you could join when you were older than 26. We notified all the other Young Farmers that were leaving the organisation at that time to let them know that there was something else they could join. The big question then was what we should call it.

I remembered that the old Norfolk word for a chat or talk was 'mardle' so I spoke to a few people who said it was a good idea and we decided to call it The Mardlers Club. I asked my woodcarver friend if he would make me a hammer and gavel and he came up with a big plaque with The Mardlers on it with a hefty wooden mallet and I presented it to the first meeting. That was how it was formed and from then on Young Farmers had something to go onto after they left the organisation in Norfolk. The Mardlers Club still meets; Henry Alston of Billockby is the chairman, and with it being the 50th anniversary in 2015 there is a dinner party for all the ex-Mardlers who were original members. We know exactly who they are because the plaque records their names, the date it was founded and the first meeting.

The Mardlers Club was founded on Wednesday, 3 March 1965 with R. Den Engelse (chairman), I. Kinloch (MAAF) as secretary and P. Bolam (MAAF) as coordinator. Founder members were A. Alston (Silfield), J. Alston (Calthorpe), W. Donald (Ridlington), B. Gaze (Diss), J. Laurie (Carleton Rode), J. Papworth (Felmingham), D. Richardson (Gt Melton), T. Tilbrook (Hardley), J. Alston Jnr (Diss), J. Askew (Wingfield), D. Drummond (Hassingham), J. Garner (Litcham), F. Oldfield (Raynham), G. Paterson (Worstead), D. Ritchie (Ludham), G. Wharton Jnr (Filby).

The first Summer Meeting was held on 19 May 1965 with a Farm Walk at Mr C. Wharton's and the first Winter Meeting was on 6 October 1965 with speaker Mr H. Plumb, now Sir Henry, at Town House Hotel. We had speakers and events but it was about socialising and though I did somehow lose touch with it after a while it is marvellous to think it is still going after half a century.

So much enjoyment came out of my connections with Young Farmers over those formative years of my life. One of the great pleasures for me was the opportunity to attend an event in May 2014 to mark the 70th anniversary of the Norfolk Federation of Young Farmers. It was held in the arena of the Royal Norfolk Showground and there was something like 1,500 people there, members who had been part of the organisation over the years, and I met up with many people I knew from the farming world in Norfolk. It was a warm late spring evening and many current members of the Norfolk clubs had helped set out the venue to ensure it was ready for the event. A member from each club also created a floral pedestal arrangement to help decorate the arena and showcase the talents within YFC. That was the way we always did things: everyone contributed, helped and got involved, and I was very pleased to see that same approach alive and well today.

Memorabilia from over the decades was also on show in the new atrium area and every guest was given a souvenir edition of the Norfolk YFC magazine. The editor, Emily Rout, had tried to create a flavour of what members over the years had loved about YFC and the doors it had opened for so many of them. She included highlights of each decade from the formation of Norfolk YFC in 1944 with 12 senior clubs affiliating. Harleston YFC was the first club to be formed, in 1938, but it was originally affiliated to Suffolk. It was a lovely evening and there was dancing and celebrations that went on into the evening. It was a fantastic event and reassuring for me to see that so many people were still involved and it was still going strong. Norfolk Young Farmers was one of the best things that happened to most young people from the farming community in Norfolk, me included.

Chapter Five

PLAYING THE PIPES

One factor which seemed to affect what happened in our lives in the most unexpected of ways was my father's health. He was very unfortunate in how he suffered with his asthma and he always seemed to be looking for a cure for his problem. He would go off to see people, so-called experts, who he thought might be able to help him recover from it. Unfortunately it was dogs and, in particular, pigs that triggered it off. There may often be no dogs in sight but he would always know instantly where there had been a dog in the house and that could start off an attack. When he went to a friend's house they would put the dog out and think it was okay but the very fact that a dog had been there was enough to start his asthma. That was something he just had to live with for the rest of his life.

We had dogs on the farm but never in the house and they were always working dogs and gun dogs, collies or Labradors. I am a firm believer in a dog being just as happy outside as dogs that are being made a fuss of but I suppose it depends if it is a working dog or not. I miss a dog, what I would like most of all is a working collie. I also had pigs before I left school but I was not too successful with them. The family had a big laugh – and probably the men on the farm did as well – when one of my sows had twins, when it should have had at least six offspring, if not 12. I decided after that that I was not going to be a pig keeper but I used to feed them myself day and night.

We suspect father's asthma may have been something to do with the cattle as well. Some of the feed for the cattle was often mixed by hand on the floor of the barn and that created a certain amount of dust. All farmers did it that way, and that is what father did for many years when he was younger and that probably triggered it off in the first place. As he got older, the thing got worse and he tried to find help for it. He would come into the house after he had been near the pigs in the early days and he would be gasping for breath. He found that lying on the floor where the air was cooler and purest was a relief, but thinking about it, it was unbelievable what he had to go through. He eventually got an inhaler which he used to help his condition. But he could not always relieve it with an inhaler and he was always going to the doctor or experts in the subject to try to get something to improve his way of life. One of those experts related to him that he should take up blowing a musical instrument, something that he had to blow through to expand and develop his lungs. Father came home and thought about it, but never took up the advice himself. However, it did give him the idea that my brother and I should learn to play an instrument, and one that we should blow into. As a Scot, he naturally thought of the bagpipes, but he never volunteered to start it off with us, though he did know a man who could teach us.

Our milk buyer, Mr Robertson (the man who ran the Co-op Dairy), was a Scot who played bagpipes for the Norfolk Caledonian Society. Father had said to him that he would like him to teach his sons to play the bagpipes. It was all set up very nicely; he would come out to the farm and talk business with father for so long and enjoy the countryside, and it was also pleasant for his wife and family, and then at some stage he would sit down with Ian and me and start to teach us on the practice chanter. As we grew more proficient, we moved on to the pipes themselves. The chanter is like a flute or recorder and that was how you practised. At that stage, we were just blowing down the practice chanter, playing a tune with the grace notes and gradually getting to know that tune by reading it off music. Eventually, we were able to play all the right notes. I'm sure Ian got on to the pipes before I did but we did it in small steps. When we got our first bagpipes we had a three-quarter set. They were easier to handle before going on to a bigger set.

When Mr Robertson came out, we would have a session and would go out onto the lawn and practise the various tunes. Often, when we stopped, we would look across to the roadside and there would be a group of people standing on the bank watching. I do remember thinking that was peculiar, having someone stand and watch us play the pipes, but it's not so long ago that a man in the village was telling me that as a boy he was among those who stood on the bank and watched us play. We had started to play before the war so I must have been quite young but I suppose it was Hitler who interrupted our bagpipe playing when we were sent away to school in Scotland.

When I came back from Scotland, Mr Robertson had moved on and taken his family to somewhere near Liverpool and was doing the same job there as he had done in Norfolk. For me, the pipes were dropped for a while but with my brother and me both back in Norfolk we discovered there was a Scottish battalion stationed at Cromer where the Pipe Major was Campbell Brown. A great big man, he had a deep voice but was friendly and he had started to play the pipes for the Norfolk

Caledonian Society. Father saw the opportunity and approached him to ask if he would be our new bagpipes teacher, which he agreed to do. He would come out to us one day a week, on a Thursday, to give us lessons. In those days, father would pick up the cash for the wages on a Thursday in North Walsham, have a cup of tea with one or two farmer friends and, as was the traditional thing, they would talk over their problems and mostly get an answer from someone in the company. Campbell Brown would catch the train to North Walsham, meet father and get a ride back with him to the house for our lesson. Later that evening, we would drive him back to Cromer. It was a routine and it was not long before we were back into the groove again with the pipes. We must have started to play quite well because it wasn't so long before we played in public. The first time that I officially played in public, or the occasion I would like to remember, was for the Norfolk Caledonian Society when I was 17. Campbell Brown led, Ian was second and I was third as we piped in the haggis for the Burns Night Dinner at the Samson and Hercules in Norwich. The three of us played, one behind the other, and he was really pleased with how we did on that night because he had put a lot of time into teaching us. Campbell Brown had a lovely manner. He made learning the bagpipes fun and was a good teacher, in fact he was an amateur piping champion and had won competitions all over Scotland, but eventually he got demobbed and disappeared back to Scotland and joined the Edinburgh Police Force and that finished that but by that time both my brother and I had learned to play quite well.

Playing on Burns Night was an experience, and as I said, it was the first time playing in public that I'd really like to remember because the time before when I played in front of people, it did not go at all well. It was while I was at Paston Grammar School in North Walsham and the plan was to have a concert made up of boys who could do things. Somebody or other got to know that I was playing the bagpipes so I was invited to take part. On the morning of the concert I took my pipes to school with me. Unfortunately, unbeknown to me, some of my fellow classmates thought it would be interesting to have a look at my bagpipes and they took them out of the box. There are three drones and the chanter reed which makes the shrill noises and a blow pipe and all were socket feeds and I think something happened and one of the reeds fell into the bag. So, when I started up to blow I could not get much noise out of the pipes because that reed had disappeared and air was escaping quicker than I could blow it in. It was all very embarrassing. I was standing on the stage red in the face with blowing but whatever I did I could not make the bagpipes work. Then the headmaster started to clap. I suppose I was not a friend to him and I got wrong by him at times. But on that day at school with my bagpipes I did appreciate his intervention because he started the clapping which meant I could get off stage and finish. I was in a bit of a flap but I learned my lesson: do not leave your pipes where people can mess with them. If you spoke to a piper at the time, he would defend his pipes with his life, and I certainly know why.

Gavin playing bagpipes.

Pipes always seemed to be with us and Ian and I played as often as we could. There was one morning, when we were on holiday in Scotland, that we found ourselves a particularly special audience, a Royal Train. At Drumclog station, near the road to Kilmarnock, there is a turning and a humpback bridge over the river. This would be during the war and we had discovered that the Royal Train would be staying there overnight. Ian and I were at the farm at Torfoot where Uncle Robert farmed and where my father used to help him before he came down to Norfolk, and we would have been visiting for the weekend. We had thought we'd go close to the train and 'wakey, wakey' the Royals on board. Ian was a bit more advanced than I was with the bagpipes at that time and he stood on the bridge and played, with me standing beside him. After a few moments a hand came out of the window and waved her handkerchief to say 'Yes, we are awake.' It was Queen Elizabeth (the Queen Mother, but she was still the Queen at the time). Many years later, I was with the Queen Mother when she came to open the new village hall at Worstead. I forgot all about asking her if she remembered being woken on the Royal Train by a boy playing the pipes.

We did have a stroke of good fortune one day a few years later in discovering a set of good quality pipes in a shop in Norwich. Campbell Brown had gone into the city with mother. She was either taking something in or had gone to fetch something and while he was waiting for her, he spied an interesting looking box at the back of this shop. It probably attracted his attention because it was a pipe box, so he wandered up to it and lifted the lid and had a dig around inside. There were lots of tartans in it but also a set of bagpipes. As he dug deeper, he found a nice silver mounted chanter. He realised that he was looking at a very good set of pipes so he asked the shopkeeper what the story behind them was and it appeared that someone had an old set of pipes that they had brought in one day. What I guess had happened was that perhaps a lady had wanted to get rid of them when her husband died and that is how they ended up in the shop. They turned out to be a really first

*Gavin (*FAR RIGHT*) playing the pipes at his sister Marion's wedding.*

class set of pipes so mother bought them there and then and that is what we learned with after that. My brother and I still played and we soon realised that when they were put together properly this was the best set of pipes we had between us. The deal was that whoever continued to play the pipes the longest would get that set of pipes. Brother played for a bit but then he got married and had a family and other things attracted him and he did not play as much but I continued to play for many more years after that, often for the Norfolk Caledonian Society, and I made sure they were never short of a piper.

The Norfolk Caledonian Society was an important part of our lives. It was for all the Scots farmers, and any Scot, who came down to Norfolk and we were always involved. My father was president, my mother was president, my brother was president, as was my sister and sister in law, and I was president twice in 1964 and 1994. It was a social gathering with annual highlights; we usually had six or more special nights throughout the year such as Hogmanay, which was obviously one of the big events of the year. We would also have a Burns Night and St Andrew's Day events and while most of the members were Scots, you did not have to be Scottish to join. The last year I was president was when I was involved in the 60th anniversary of the forming of the Norfolk Caledonian Society because they wanted someone from a family which had been there from the word go. That year we raised £5,000 for the Norfolk Leukaemia Fund. Father was one of the instigators of the Caledonian Society and he had helped set it up. It wasn't, however, the only organisation for Scots. There was also the Norwich St Andrew's Society, which was more made up of solicitors and accountants, the town folk. I remember some 20 years ago at our AGM, the chairman reported that a letter had been received from the St Andrew's Society suggesting that the two societies should get together, which I thought would not be a bad idea and eventually that is what happened.

As a piper, it was good for me to play for the Norfolk Caledonian Society at events and on other special occasions because I had to keep practising and there was a need to keep the bagpipes in good order otherwise all the reeds and the workings inside get dried out. That is critical so it is better to keep playing them twice a week or something like that. Anything less and it is a big job to get them tuned up again; once you let it slip you are not going to play it as well as someone who would play the pipes regularly. I was an Honorary Piper for the Norfolk Caledonian Society for over 40 years.

There was a time in my life that I always seemed to be playing the bagpipes. If it wasn't for friends at their functions, weddings or with the Caledonian Society, it was with my Uncle Rob's Anglo-Scots Concert Party. Rob, my mother's brother, farmed at Witton and Crostwight and he was a great one for putting on parties for people and Aunt Belle could always do a great spread. There were tennis parties, even beach parties as he lived near the coast, and there would often be a crowd of the Flemings come up from Sussex, and people there from Norfolk and Scotland.

Rob could sing. In fact he could sing really well, but he had an unfortunate

Kilted and booted for a family wedding:
LEFT TO RIGHT *unknown, Gavin, unknown, Billy Ritchie, Ian, cousin Lindsay.*

childhood with illness and accident. When Rob was a boy, you could get from the house – where my mother lived – straight through into the cowshed. There used to be a bin full of bran mash for the cows, it was a laxative to make sure the cows were not tight in their bowels and it was good for them because they would eat more and the more they ate, the more milk they produced. To make up this mix, the family would put boiling water into the bin. Before they fed the cows they would let it cool and then give it to the cattle. Uncle Rob used to go through from the house and on his way by he would plunge his arms into the bran tub and play with it. But one day he did it with the boiling water in and it scalded his arms up to the elbow. Later in his youth, he had double pneumonia twice and did not go to school much. Because some of the problem was with his chest, he was encouraged to sing. That seemed to be what was always suggested in those days, so he decided to learn to sing.

Being a Scot, he had the same accent as the famous Harry Lauder and he used to sing a lot of Harry's songs. Lauder was the first man to put on record 1,000 songs and I even got to shake his hand one night when he was in Norwich. Father took us to see him in his changing room and we were quite thrilled to meet him though I'm not so sure he felt the same. We do, however, have something of Harry Lauder with us in the family today. He lived at a place he called Lauder Hall, which was just on the outskirts of Strathaven, and there was a sale of his possessions, probably not that long after he died, and we have a cabinet from that sale. It was one of the artefacts from his house, it's a fine piece of furniture and we now have it at Holly House.

At around that time at the Caledonian Society there was a man called Tom Stuart. He was a travelling salesman for the bacon factory at Bury St Edmunds and would go all over the place and go round the shops in the villages in Norfolk and knew the shopkeepers well. A lot of them were involved in events in their village and he knew a lot about them as his customers.

Uncle Rob had formed the Anglo-Scots Concert Party towards the end of the war with Tom, another broad Scot, who was the organiser and MC. His customers would often ask him if he would bring it along to their events to help them make some money for good causes in their area. Uncle Rob was the singer and he would put his kilt on and sing all the famous songs and when I eventually joined I would play the pipes in my kilt as well, it was a very colourful affair. In the days before I joined they had found a dancer in Norwich who could dance the Highland Fling and the Sword Dance and when I came along I started playing the pipes for her to dance to. There was also a concert pianist who played for Uncle Rob and Bill Cullum, who was a comedian. We played in village halls and we all were willing to do it for charity; everybody liked it and Uncle Rob loved doing it. He was a good singer but he would much rather sing to a small audience for charity than go on to a big stage but he could have earned his living by singing. He was a wonderful singer and could sing all the songs made popular by Harry Lauder very well indeed. We were helping old people and young people for charity and supporting those who needed things for their community.

That was good for me because it gave me enough practice to keep the pipes in tune and ensure I was never running out of puff. Blowing and playing for the Caledonian Society and the Concert Party kept things ticking over nicely for me. The concert party went on for a number of years and we were happy to do it if we were invited along to events. I still love the sound of bagpipes and I thoroughly enjoyed learning to play them and playing them at so many events over the years. I don't play them now, but I still have that special set of pipes discovered at the back of a shop in Norwich by Pipe Major Campbell Brown to this day.

The Anglo-Scots Concert Party.

Chapter Six

TAKING UP THE REINS

Father had become very ill. He had suffered with asthma for most of his life but this was much more serious and very worrying for us all. He had an ulcerated stomach and was really under the weather. When I think about it, I can understand why he perhaps became ill with all the things he had on his plate. He knew he needed to get it sorted out but every year he liked to go up to Scotland with his brother-in-law – Uncle Rob – though the doctors weren't so keen. They wanted him to go into hospital fairly quickly for an operation. Dad, however, was determined. He told the doctors he would be going to Scotland but would go into hospital on his return. They warned him that if he was unfortunate enough to have his stomach spring a leak, it would be serious, but dad decided to go anyway. Father was under no illusions and he knew perfectly well that he would need an operation. He did go to Scotland and all worked out well and then when he came back, went into the Norfolk and Norwich Hospital for surgery.

It was not a good time for father. Once he came out of hospital and was recovering he had a rough period where he just could not get his stomach to work again after having the operation. Perhaps that was no real surprise considering they had actually taken as much as seven-eighths of his stomach away. As he got stronger, the idea was that he should eat little but often, to try to get his digestive system working again. Father was struggling with that, something wasn't going right, but the solution came from the most unusual and unexpected source. Jack Crawford was someone we knew from the Norfolk Caledonian Society. A Scot, he was the manager of the chocolate factory in Norwich and one day called in to see how father was getting along.

'Not too well at all,' father told him. 'My stomach won't start working again and even though I have tried tablets to get things moving, nothing seems to be happening.'

Father was desperate but Mr Crawford had a bright idea. He asked father, 'Have you tried a sherry called Fino Benito? It moves most things.'

'Never heard of it,' said father, but he was that anxious to get back to normal he told his fellow Scot that he'd go out and get a bottle straight away, which he duly did. Dad took a sip of this sherry and in his words, 'All of a sudden I had the most wonderful feeling in my stomach and things began to happen.'

I would say that is possibly what saved his life. From then on, father had to be careful what he ate and how he ate but he did start to improve. That reminds me, when I was ill many years later and needed an operation, my sister went out and bought me a bottle of Fino Benito, just in case!

In the years before his illness and as Ian and I got older, father had started to think about the two of us moving more into the management of the farms. The war was still going on when I came home from Scotland and though I remember the end of it, life on the farm went on much as usual and I learned more and more about what was going on. Our time was tied up with cattle simply because of our milk cows and we knew how to feed them and look after them, that was ingrained into us at an early age and we were really the spare herdsmen that went from farm to farm to help when required.

It was at about this time that Ian was ready to move into farming in his own right. Being older than I, he had attended the agricultural college in Scotland a few years prior to me. While he was there he went visiting with our cousin Gavin Alston from Sco Ruston, who had relations in Fife. It was there he met Elsie and by the time he was 21 and back home, she had become his wife and they were living at Hall Farm, Dilham. I was still at home and 18, though very involved in the farm. With Ian settling down, Dad was keen that he should get started on his own.

'If you are going to get married, you had better take on one of the farms,' Dad said to him.

Ian, though, caught father by surprise. He said he would like to have Hall Farm, Dilham, which was the farm that father had bought most recently. I could understand that: the house was a bit special and Ian thought Elsie would like it as well and between them they had decided it was the farm they would like to take.

That set father aback a bit. He said to Ian, 'Yes, but that is my new toy.' Mother then stepped in and they began having a discussion which may have got into an argument if it went much further. As usual, I was listening but mother said to father, 'The boy wants to get started in farming, let him get on with it.' So Ian went to Dilham Hall. I remember that distinctly because I agreed with him. If he was going to get started in farming he needed to go where he wanted to be in order to be happy.

Ian and I always got on well together, we used to fall out when we were boys as all youngsters do but nothing serious and when Ian married Elsie and they started having babies, I used to love going up there and seeing them just before they were put to bed.

While Ian was getting settled in to running his own farm, I was content learning about lots of different things about farming and the trades associated with it. I remember that I did a winter at a garage workshop and it was good to get to know that job. The venture – Gleave and Key – was run by Wesley Key, who had a butcher's shop as well as running a farm, and his partner was Snowy Gleave. What they did was get me an old butcher's van to demolish. It stank to high heaven of stale meat and was due for scrap. They told me to tear that old van to bits, take all the pieces out and then put it back together again and start it up. It was a smelly old job but I learned a huge amount from that and I was grateful for the opportunity and I saw for myself all the things that were happening within the business and how they did things. It was a garage workshop and as farmers we would get together and give it a lot of business. Mr Key ran the farm and Snowy ran the workshop. I got to know Mr Gleave and when I started farming he would ring me up at about ten in the morning and ask if I was doing anything. I'd say, 'Nothing in particular.'

'Would you like a coffee? The pot is on the boil at my house, come over in five minutes and it'll be ready,' he'd say.

Over I'd ride and we'd have a good time talking about different things over a coffee. I'm sure he'd usually have something on his mind but after that he'd feel better. I did enjoy his company on those mornings we had coffee together but he was sadly killed one night walking his dog. I was out shooting the next day when I heard. It was very sad and a great shock to me.

When it came to my turn to get more into the management side of farming, having seen Ian making a success up at Hall Farm, I gravitated towards Manor Farm at Worstead. It started off quite steady; I'd get up in the morning and father would give me orders to take to the foreman Billy Smith about what he wanted the men to do. He would probably talk to the foreman about it himself too but he passed the messages on to me and I took them to Worstead in that way for the best part of a year. In my mind at the time it was an experiment to see if I could do the job. I was confident I could get through it but I remember thinking that the more I got into it, the more I would have to record everything properly. As time went by I gradually played a bigger role in the management of Manor Farm at Worstead.

As a farming business, we were heavily involved with the Westwick factory which was freezing peas. We had formed a farmers group and, within that, mostly the younger people in the group took on the role as acting managers or foremen and we each did a stint. The factory was running round the clock and we would do

12 hours each when we were in charge. One night shift stands out in particular for me; it had been a terrible night because the land was sticky with the rain and the machinery kept getting stuck and breaking down but it was more than that because that night marked a change in the way I lived, virtually from then on really. We struggled through at the pea factory, we managed to keep the machinery going on that night in question right through until the early morning. I was due to come home to Smallburgh, to Holly House for breakfast, where I lived with mother and father still. Work was going on over at Holly Grove, Worstead, where the house was being prepared for me to move into as that was now the estate house for Manor Farm. The Army had left Manor Farm House and we had taken it back after they used it during the war but it was sold and Holly Grove was the new farmhouse. That particular pea shift was a stinker. I was covered in muck and thought to myself that if I was to go on to Smallburgh I would be in trouble going into the house in such a state so I went to Holly Grove, had a shower and got into bed. I rang the foreman up at Smallburgh as I knew he would be speaking to father and said to tell him I should be up for breakfast later. That was the start of my life at Holly Grove and I never slept anywhere else after that. I took that house as my own, until I moved into Holly House at Church Farm, Smallburgh, after mother died many years later. I moved in to Holly Grove as a single man and had one of the men's wives, Mrs Howton, who used to 'do' for me but I still came up to Church Farm for my breakfast every morning and to look at the mail. I'd eat by myself later in the day at Holly Grove or would be out somewhere or pick something up later. That was how I moved out of the family home and started to take on full responsibility for the farm. But I didn't do so badly after all and by year end I had come up with a profit, so I was happy. That was the launch of me in business as a farmer, in 1951, at the age of 21.

While this was happening, our sister Marion was growing up. She went to Eastbourne to a Dow School where she was taught to cook and she got a job at The London Hospital cooking. She was slim with golden hair and later married another Scot, David Laurie Richie, in 1958 and had a girl named Marion in line with family tradition and a boy named Laurie.

Manor Farm was roughly 540 acres and some of it was light land, almost sand. We had a herd of 72 cows, as we did on each of the four farms, and we later used the sand to bed cows but other than that it was quite good land. We chucked muck on the fields from the cows, as we did on all the farms, and that was what gave it the fertility. The fields that were nearer the cowsheds were the ones that had more fertility than some of the others. If you had cows, sheep or bullocks, the old English system was to fatten cattle to get muck. But the difference between fattening cattle and milking cows was that you got a cheque once a month for the milk as well as the muck to spread on the land. That is a fact and father based his farming on that system.

We needed about one acre of pasture per cow and we had about 100 acres in those days and they would eat it all. Every day in summer time they went out of the shed to pasture but in the winter they slept in. We'd also feed them cattle cake which gave them a balanced ration; so they produced milk, calved and were milked twice a day. On the fields, there was rotation with wheat, barley, oats and peas for the factory as a cash crop and sugar beet and potatoes. It was a standard farm but we always used the by-products for the cows. For instance, the sugar beet tops, which in those days were cut by hand, were used to feed the cattle. We grew mangel and they were solely for feeding to the cattle, along with rolled oats to supplement the feeding ration. We were rearing 30–70 heifer calves each year and probably did not need them all so we sold some when they were getting close to calving. We had been selling cattle at certain times of year for a while; sometimes calf heifers, sometimes cows that had calved and we had quite a business selling cattle as well as breeding them.

We were still in the horse era, of course, though we had tractors as well. The tractor had been part of the business since father farmed at Rushall in the 1930s. We still had eight horses in the stable when I took over and there might have been two tractors but more were coming in fast. Young people, including me, liked tractors. Sitting on a tractor and driving it was a lot better than walking behind a pair of horses but that was just progress. Originally, I was keen on horses, they were fantastic animals on the farm, and I suppose until we started showing the cattle, my favourites were the horses but once we showed it was the cows that I favoured all the time.

I hadn't been on my own in charge of Manor Farm for that long when father became ill. His illness, subsequent operation and a period of recovery saw him unable to play any real role in the business for some time and it fell to Ian and me to keep the four farms running: Manor Farm, Worstead; Church Farm, Smallburgh; Manor Farm, Dilham; and Hall Farm, Dilham – run as four separate businesses, each with its own labour, a foreman in charge and each with its own dairy herd of 72 cows. When father was in hospital, Ian was farming at Dilham Hall. It was natural that he should take over the management of Dilham Manor and I took over the management of Smallburgh with Worstead. To be fair, all the farms had a good foreman which made it quite easy for us to keep them running as before.

Between leaving hospital and coming home, father spent time in a nursing home on Newmarket Road in Norwich. Some of the time father was not entirely with it; he could speak but he was not thinking clearly. He was delirious. That was the most difficult thing to handle but that was the sort of thing that happened after an operation like the one he had. He could remember the fields of the farm but he was telling me that the crops would be ready when I knew for certain that they were not. I was able to talk to him but I was never too sure what answer I would get because his mind was wandering. For a few days we had to put up with that from him, then it disappeared and he began to get better and eventually he came home. I was working hard trying to keep the farms running and meet my Young Farmers' commitments as well as going to the meetings on a Tuesday night and visit Dad in the nursing home. I didn't have much time to myself, apart from going out for a meal with friends on a Saturday night. Perhaps that is when I began to think about taking opportunities that might come my way and what had led to that meeting at Downham Market.

As father got better, he eventually took back the management of his two farms and left Ian to manage Dilham Hall and me with Manor Farm, Worstead, as was originally intended. We knew what we had to do, though it wasn't always straightforward. We knew the men well but a young man like myself appearing on the scene did cause a few problems. Some of the men were trying me out, trying to impress their authority on me when I was trying to impress my authority on them but we gradually sorted it all out. There were extreme personalities and in some cases it was very much a case of knowing the personality and how to get that man on your side. There was one who was a clever mechanic. He did a lot of machinery repairs and replacement, was knowledgeable at his job – which we appreciated – and under normal circumstances he was very easy to talk to. However, I did know that if you let rip into him and squared him up in a big way, he would go off in a huff for about a month. There was another man whom I got to know very well. They were both nice characters but the second man was the sort that if you went up to him to gently advise him to do better, he would not do as he was told; you almost had to give him firm direction and then he would do a much better job. I think I learned a lot of lessons from these two because both were extreme examples but both were good men. We had a lot of very good men on the farm for many years.

Father still had a lot of input and it was he who had chosen the foremen and he was very good at choosing a foreman. Some were better in certain ways than others. With the four units, the four farms – which were all very similar – we worked as a team and never more so than at harvest time. Harvest wasn't over until all four farms were finished. If one of them finished, those that were finished immediately went to help with the amount that was left which was a wonderful thing because all of a sudden you doubled up your gang. Sometimes that happened a lot if we got behind or there was a bigger harvest to do. When we helped each other there was no money changed hands, we just switched the gang over and helped finish that farm. It was wonderful, you always worried about getting through as you did not want to be last to finish but that did relieve the pressure if you were getting too late for harvest, knowing help was at hand. Your harvest is the production part of the year, the important part of the year. You worked hard at other things during the year and got things ready but when it came to harvesting you did not bugger that up.

Father had set things up very well; the men liked working for us, they all liked getting things done well and they liked working with each other. I was quite relieved that I turned in a profit on the first year because it was an unknown quantity to me. Father had been very kind to Ian and me, kinder than we probably thought at the time. When we first started farming on our own, he kept his distance but he kept his eye on us too.

On his weekly trips to pick up the wages money from North Walsham on a Thursday, he'd make good use of the journey. On his way there, he would go one way which took him by Worstead. On the way back, he came another way which went through Dilham. From his car he would see everything that he needed to see about the two farms, everything that was wrong. But he had a way of telling us, he would never say straight out that he thought it was all a bloody mess. But we got to know the way he was thinking. He would ask us what we had in such and such a field and we'd tell him.

'Oh,' he'd say, 'I couldn't see it. It's not growing very well.'

He was pretty kind to us and when I think about it, I can see that he had always played it through in his mind long before he said anything to us. Ian was settled at Dilham with Elsie before I started farming but father seldom went back to their farm until he was invited. He did not want to interfere with them as a couple. Father always said to us that we could turn to him for guidance, but what he was also saying was, 'Come back to me for advice if you need it but I shall not be poking my nose in.'

Father had built these farms up and then handed them over to us and allowed us to get on with it. And that was a wonderful thing.

Chapter Seven

Mrs Bugg's Smile

On one particular morning father was uptight. In fact, I don't ever recall him being so tense and uncertain about what to do. He was going down to London, supposedly to talk about buying the Worstead Estate, and I went with him. He had thought long and hard about buying it and no doubt talked it over with those whose judgement and advice he trusted: our accountant and solicitor, perhaps his closest friends and some relations.

Sir Harold Harmsworth had died in 1952 when we had the four farms, those we rented off the Worstead Estate and Church Farm at Smallburgh. Ian was already established in the farming game and starting his family with Elsie at Dilham while I was just about through my first challenging, albeit finally profitable, first year as a farmer in my own right at Manor Farm, Worstead and now settled in to Holly Grove. In the three or four years after Harmsworth's death, the estate seemed to change hands two or three times and this wasn't particularly helpful to us as the sitting tenants.

Father was over the worst of his illness but he wasn't the man he had been before his operation and he was not too happy with the situation concerning the estate. He was complaining. He was fed up with the ongoing state of affairs and frustrated with the changing ownership. If we wanted to request the estate owner to repair something on the estate, because that was their responsibility and something which unfortunately happened fairly regularly, we had a rigmarole to go through. To do that we had to talk to the local agent who would talk to the agent who was selling it and he would talk to somebody representing someone who was probably lying on their death bed, all of which was not very efficient. And father was getting fed up with it because we had constantly changing landlords. The agent that was trying to sell it must have got wind of his feelings and it came as little surprise when he eventually said to father, 'Why don't you buy it?'

Father told him he was not really ready to buy. 'I don't think I could do that,' he replied.

We were always in touch with the agent, and while the selling agent was a different agent to ours they were all connected and involved in the deal in one way or another. Buying, however, was not in the mind of many farmers and there was usually a good reason for that. If you did not like the farm where you were, you just moved on by giving notice; that was the normal procedure. But by the time all this happened father had already got land in this area and he liked being in Worstead and Smallburgh because of the quality of the land. If you lease the land, you have to pay rent; if you buy it, you do not have to pay rent and if you can buy it and can make ends meet, that is one bill you do not have to pay. Rents, however, were not huge and that may have been one reason why, despite the Worstead Estate coming up for sale every so often, father was still not that interested in buying it. He felt he already owned enough land.

With Manor Farm, Dilham, and Manor Farm, Worstead, on the estate and rented by us, we were the sitting tenant which did give us a much better chance of buying it if father did start to think along those lines. We were already farming two-thirds of the estate and there was some appeal to buying the land and farming it under ownership. There were also a number of other much smaller farms on the estate. Eventually, having weighed up this scenario and being fed up with constantly changing landlords, father must have thought again about buying the estate – more seriously than before – and started to slowly put things in place for that. Having four farms that were working well and were separately run by four farming companies with separate accounts made our position stronger. I think we talked to the accountant and he would have said that if you get four farms with four companies, each can borrow money. Father followed that advice and I suppose you have to say that his record of making things pay was pretty good and the banks went with it and agreed it was a good thing. Something I cannot emphasise enough is the model of a monthly cheque coming in from milk production, because it was the key to father's success.

We were very, very lucky with our accountant and solicitor and that was by listening to other people who would say there was a good man in that firm and a good man in the other firms and we are still with those two firms. If you get the right advice at the right time, that takes you forward nicely. Father would have talked through what he had already bought, Church Farm and Dilham Hall, with the accountant, but the estate was a lot more money than either of them and he was worried that he could not afford that. The thought of buying it was a dangerous thing to do. Most farmers were scared to borrow money and the banks were scared to lend as well because of the fluctuation in prices. I suppose, as we got more and more involved in the world market, prices were unpredictable and still are.

Traditionally, estates would let their land but if you wanted land you had to buy it when it was for sale. This kept changing according to the atmosphere in this business but at that time there was a lot of uncertainty. While father was content that he had enough land bought already, he also had two sons in Ian and me who wanted to get set up in farming. He was talking to other people in the family about what to do and I suspect he was thinking to himself that this was quite an opportunity if it would work. But that was the issue: could he make it work?

At the time a lot of farmers were not doing well and people were getting into all sorts of trouble but with all the people father was talking to, something must have changed his view and made him begin to think more about buying the estate and in a very serious way. Eventually, he made up his mind that was what he would do.

The day arrived when father went to London, with me in tow, ready to buy the Worstead Estate. He was as nervous as I'd seen him, but it went to plan and he believed he had a deal and returned home with that in his head. The next day, the phone rang and it was the agent. It was bad news, news that took father by surprise. From thinking he had a deal, father suddenly found that was not the case.

'We have had to put the price up because there was another buyer who had come onto the scene who wants to buy it,' the agent told him. 'If you still want the estate, I think you will have to bid a little higher.'

This was where father was grateful he had someone like Uncle James to turn to for advice and he gave him a call. We all knew Uncle James, as did all the Scots in Norfolk. He had a reputation, a good reputation, and was a man with a lot of common sense and a nice attitude to life. I can remember him very well, he had a wonderful deep voice, he did not speak very quickly but you knew that what he said he meant and he did say what he thought.

He had been here some years before father came down to Norfolk. There was a Scottish tradition in farming families: the eldest son got the first chance to farm; the second son would also usually be set up on a farm, and the youngest son had to launch out on his own and go and look for what he could find. Uncle James was that younger son, so first he went to Canada and had a look and then came back to settle in Suffolk in 1903. From there, he decided to move to Norfolk, farming at Uphall, and some years after that, father came down. As mother's brother, James was well placed for father to call on for advice. He also knew all the agents quite well and he knew how to advise people. It was only natural, at such a time as this and with so much at stake, for father to consult Uncle James Alston.

What had upset father was that when he came home to Norfolk from the meeting in London, he was thinking that he had bought the estate. And then he received the message to say there had been another bid for it, more than he had bid, and something that he had to take note of and work on. Father wondered if it was a ploy to just try to push him to pay more as I don't think he trusted that agent too well. When he came off the phone from Uncle James, he had a clearer idea of what he would do.

Uncle James told him, 'Neither you, nor anyone else, can value that land within the difference in price. If it was worthy of buying before, I do not think that should stop you buying it now.'

In reality the uplift in price was not a huge amount of money, so Dad rang the agent and said he would bid a bit more. It was accepted and we became the owners of Worstead Estate, all 1,757 acres of it, as we still are today. Some months later we discovered it was the Royal Family that had also bid and led to father bidding more. If he had chosen not to, we might have had the Worstead Estate being owned by royalty.

When the dust had settled father began to think he had bought it at a good price. Looking at it now, the thing that I am flabbergasted over is that we had paid an amount that was so much per acre throughout the estate with the price including the woods, the cottages, farm buildings and farm houses. Nowadays if you were buying a farm you would buy the land and then start to buy the houses if you wanted them. It meant we now farmed the whole of the Worstead Estate, with tenant farmers in some of the other farms. The big house had gone but there was Holly Grove, where Harmsworth lived and where I used to live. As a property, Holly Grove actually had a long history. It was quite old and has a Georgian frontage, which was added at some stage. One of the people who lived there in the 1920s was a Lieutenant-Colonel Besant who had fought with Lord Kitchener in Egypt.

The property side of things was what father worried about right from the word go because the 40 cottages on the Worstead Estate we had acquired were in a poor state of repair and were not worth any money at that time. There was a mix of cottages in terms of size, appearance and garden space and we knew a lot of work needed doing as regards electricity, toilets and generally improving them for the cottagers. There hadn't been a lot of maintenance done on the cottages, particularly when the landlord was changing so often, so we set about trying to correct that with any profit we had from the farm to help benefit the tenants and the properties they lived in. When we think about it now, there were so many things that needed doing with them that it was a case of what should we do first but in time, an awful lot of modernising was done to improve the properties. It usually had a bill with it but when we were finished we had places that were worth something.

The other factor to consider was that when we bought the estate most of the people living in the cottages were working on the farms. If they retired, they could stay in them but didn't have much money and probably couldn't pay their rent. That was the truly frightening part of the deal. Former estate workers were entitled to live there until they died but most were sound country people and while the people living in them were poor, they kept them as well as they could. If you got a good family in, usually quite a big family with four or five children with a man who had good common sense and a wife who worked hard, those were the people we knew we should be employing on the farm. Their gardens, I recall, were always immaculate, well-maintained and in crop all the time.

We probably talked the situation through with our accountant and tried to get some idea of the economics of our cottage properties; we tried to think about what we could do with them to make them better, what we could charge in rent if we got them to that stage and what they really would be worth. Farming was probably making money but we did not want to spend it if we were not going to get anything back. One of the first things we did when we bought the estate was survey the cottages. We would call on the people who lived in them and have a chat; on some occasions that was difficult but not that often.

We discovered that most cottagers were paying very little and in one case, I found that we were virtually paying a tenant to live in her home because she was paying so little in rent and we were paying more to maintain the property. I realised I had to go and see this lady and work out if I could get an understanding with her, though I didn't exactly look forward to the meeting. She was one of the people we sold fruit to when Ian and I were boys. She would always buy from us and had a smile and welcomed us to the door, so I already had a good relationship with her and I think I was lucky from that point of view. She was a middle-aged woman, it was only a small cottage and she lived there alone but it was a good little cottage and she was perfectly happy. I knocked on her door and I was, I am sure, flushed in the face.

'I've come to see about your rent,' I told her as she answered.

Mrs Bugg looked me in the eyes and gave me that big beaming smile she used to give me all those years before when Ian and I turned up on her doorstep with our punnets of raspberries and blackcurrants.

'I wondered how long it would be before you came by to see me,' she said.

She had done her figures as well and had been expecting me for some time. We talked it through in a very friendly way, we came to an arrangement and she was happy enough. All was fine and I was pleased it had gone that way because she was a lovely lady. On the whole, most tenants were happy to see me. I have to say that if they thought we were going to do things for them, they were only too pleased to talk.

We may not have fully realised it, but as time went by these cottages have become an exceptional asset. Some might have seen them as a nuisance, but we feel they have turned out to be of direct value. It landed on our plate but is now diversification from our core farm business. In those early days, the farm side supported the cottages by providing us with the money to put into them and improve them but that has now turned round and we have money coming from the cottages to enable us to do things on the farm. Now, we also have six barn conversions and some of them are really grand houses. But back then, when we first took over the estate, it was about doing the basics to improve the cottages for those who lived in them.

The Worstead Estate also came with a lot of woodland, which left us with work to do on the forestry side and we are looking at doing more now. With forestry you get some usable timber. We have a wood yard where we cut planks to make gates, though now we are moving towards iron gates. There is not exactly a lot of money to be made from timber growing but we do like to keep our woodland in trim. Planting is not cheap but we did a lot of that in the early years, perhaps 60 years ago now when we first bought the estate, planting trees in the walled garden so they were protected from the rabbits and deer, which would eat them. The walled garden was a good place to start growing trees before planting them out on the estate. We got to the stage where a lot of the timber was being thinned

Unmodernised cottages at Worstead in the 1930s.

to make posts for the farm and while we have thinned the trees, we have still got plenty left. It is about progressive forestry management. We bought the estate with a long-term vision and, however you look at it, we must be thankful father saw it like that. When he took it on, who was to know that the cottages were going to be worth any money?

We did a lot of other work on Worstead Park over the years with the woodland, or laying the concrete road, which was a big job in itself. One of the jobs was to improve the lake and clean it out though we did dredge up more than we bargained for. The lake had a lot of trees growing around it; some would be better not there and others looked very nice. We took it on to tidy up the lake and talked to someone about dredging it as they said they had a machine that would do that job. The machine to dredge the lake was on a boat and it was a funny contraption. It was a bit like a combine but on a different scale. You dropped the machine over the end of the boat and let it go down to the bottom of the lake. The head had a roller which sucked the mud and debris into a pump and everything went in except the branches of trees. This boat could also deal with them as well and had a winch which you could use to put a wire rope round the tree and lift it out of the water. The mud that was sucked up was pumped through a pipe, which floated on the surface and went to the bank and then further into the trees and pumped the mud out in a suitable place such as in the wood. The mud would run about among the trees and find its own level and that was how we got rid of it. The lake was dredged because it was silting up and just needed cleaning.

It was mostly mud in the lake but there was one day when the machine stopped suddenly and there was something stuck in the header. It was rattling away as it sucked but when it stopped we had to lift it out and have a look at what the problem was. Stuck in there was a World War Two hand grenade. We knew the Army had been camped on the park during the war in 30–40 huts and I think it was a case that if they had anything they didn't want to take away with them they just slung it in the lake and the grenade was one of those items. But if it had gone off when we dredged it up, there would have been a clatter.

Anyway, once we had discovered it was a hand grenade we carefully removed it and put it in the back of my truck to take it home for the bomb disposal people to come and deal with it, though I wasn't that comfortable with it. Thankfully, it didn't go off. When they arrived they took a look at it and said that it was never going to go off and from our point of view that was good, very good. I suppose having thrown it in the back of the truck, if it was going to go off that was the time. We also found some grenades on the edge of the bank and that was something that could have been worse. Although I brought it home and handled it carefully, it was a bit

*Gamekeeper Frank Anderton (*RIGHT*) with the author's father beside the lake.*

scary because you are never sure about those things. That must have been 30 or more years ago. Having dredged the lake it made a big difference and we noticed after that we got more wild birds and water birds come in so it did some good. The park is a funny place and you find a lot of wildlife in there and see at close quarters the habits of birds and that can be very interesting to observe.

Worstead Park is the golden plum of our property and land. It would have been in about 2010 that we looked closely at how we could make even better use of it and we did apply to build a hotel on it. Where the big house that Harmsworth demolished once stood, there was an old coach house. It was the work of well known architect James Wyatt, who had also built the house at the end of the eighteenth century. Unfortunately, the coach house had fallen into a bad state of repair and we needed to do something about it. We started to think it through and had several ideas. One of them came to me a few years before that when I was travelling around the country in my role as President of the Holstein Society. I stayed in a lot of hotels that were disappointing and saw nothing that I would like to have seen in Worstead Park, which I did think was a perfect place to have a really well-designed hotel that would serve North Norfolk.

We had plans drawn up and applied to North Norfolk District Council. At the first meeting they said they did not like the plans so we went off to think how we could make them better. The second set of plans were beautiful and drawn up by an architect from this area. The design incorporated the coach house and the arches in a hotel that had about 30 rooms. Many of the councillors thought it was lovely but wanted to see the site so they decided to have a site meeting.

In the meantime, English Heritage started to show an interest and had a look on the site, albeit without our permission, and made comments, noting that an old stable was involved, which I had pointed out was not in very good order. I went to the next meeting of the council after that and the English Heritage man was there. The councillors were saying what a lovely site it was and I thought that we might have got permission but the English Heritage man had another view.

He said, 'I am sorry to say that you are imitating an old style building and you can't do that.'

It irritated me to see that one person's opinion, when the council would have been happy to see it happen, stopped the whole plan particularly when it was my money that I was spending. With the English Heritage man saying he could not support the plan, I asked if he would help and tell me what style he thought would suit the site.

The coach house.

'It's not my job to do that,' he retorted, and was not at all helpful, even though it was his point of view that had seen the plans turned down. I said to him privately afterwards that it would be a big help if he could offer some guidance but if it was my money I am spending, I would have to like it as well. He would not give us any help at all and North Norfolk District Council could not pass the plans. That took the steam out of me as regards developing the Worstead Estate in this way.

The Worstead Estate is still a wonderful area; there are muntjac and red deer and we run a shoot with pheasants, partridge, ducks and the odd woodcock. We have got some high woods and if you come across a good shot, he would want the challenge of his birds flying high. As a family we have shot on the estate and it was always a lot of fun and the characters that would come along would have a really good day out. We now have someone who organises the shooting for us and we want to see it continue because it is part of country life that you cannot ignore. What never ceases to amaze me though is that this part of North Norfolk, now very much part of our land and our farming estate, might have been Crown property, owned by the Royal Family, if father had made a different decision all those years ago.

Chapter Eight

SMALLBURGH BRENDA –
SUPREME CHAMPION

Father was keen to hear my impressions of the Dairy Show. It was 1952 and I'd gone down to London on a bus trip with some friends to see and experience the show, which at that time was the biggest event of the year for dairy farmers. He was sitting up in bed with a cup of tea when I took the mail and the morning paper up to him. While still recovering from his operation, he was a lot better and starting to think about getting more involved in the business again, though you could say he was half the man he was. He weighed near on 16 stone when he went into hospital but after his surgery and recuperation, he was little more than seven stones in weight. Father wasn't a man for showing cattle and we didn't have a pedigree herd, though we had just bought our first four pedigree heifers. But he knew all the breeders' names with the Ayrshires and British Friesians, so he wanted a full report and all the detail of everything that went on. I told him about the bus trip, which was a group of us from the Aylsham Young Farmers' Club and had been organised by Matthew Mitchell of Blickling with his sons, and then I talked him through who had won the various classes and who was there and what had gone on. If you had lived in Scotland for any length of time and you were interested in cows, going to shows was the key to getting to know people and so he was very interested. I discussed the cattle and told him which breeders had done well and then left him with a final remark, though at the time I had no idea where it would lead.

'There were some very good cows at the show,' I said to father as he picked up the morning paper, 'but we have cows in that shed out there that are just as good as those which performed well at the Dairy Show.'

I nodded over to the cowshed across the yard, not really expecting any comment from father. But as I turned to leave him to the paper and his post, he looked up and said, 'If you really think that, talk to George and pick out some to trial out and see what you can get out of them.'

George Clare was the herdsman (a fine herdsman at that) and his son Arthur followed in the same vein and became my herdsman eventually and we all worked well together. They were both very knowledgeable men on handling cows; father, and I in turn, respected their opinion. The plan was to pick out two cows that were fresh-calved and see how they performed with a view to getting them ready for the following year's Dairy Show. We picked Lavenham Cherry, which was one of the four pedigree heifers we had bought, and Smallburgh Brenda from our own breeding herd. Father was not that keen on the pedigree side himself, he just liked good cows, but when he saw how interested Ian and I had become in cows, he decided to buy some pedigree Ayrshire and Friesian cows and that was the start of our pedigree breeding, which has continued ever since. In 1953 Lavenham Cherry was a good pedigree Friesian. There was one that did not do so well out of the four but the other three left good families in the herd. Lavenham Cherry 19th, as registered in the Holstein Society herd book, has the prefix Lavenham and is the 19th of her family and was a typical pedigree Holstein.

For the Dairy Show, the key was how much milk they would produce and how the cows would react to getting so much special attention and food. We needed to know, if we entered them for the Dairy Show, how they would perform and more importantly how would they perform on the day. While it was father's comment that started it, he knew how important it was to work with George and put it to the test.

'There are show cows, and there are show cows,' he said.

What he meant was that if your cows are reactive by nature then you are in with a chance of doing well but if she fights against all the attention they can be difficult to handle. I was cock-a-hoop with the idea but I was not sure that I knew enough about it. As luck would have it, Brenda was exceptional. We knew she was good but we did not quite know how good she was and what her reaction would be. But she was a docile creature and happy to go with it but that is partly down to the herdsman as well. However, while Brenda was a good choice from our point of view, not everyone thought that much of her. She was a supplementary pedigree Friesian and it annoyed some people to think she was not a pure bred full pedigree. Her pedigree only went back two generations. To us, it did not mean very much, she was just a cow that would do that job. However, so-called perfectionists were saying she should not even be at the show, but to us that just showed that pure breeding is not always the answer.

George and I set to work with Brenda. She was fed three times a day and milked three times a day and went on it straight away and so we decided she would do. Father also brought in an in-calf heifer from one of the best herds to see how she turned out but she did not like to be handled. The key to the Dairy Show was in the timing: you have to get the cow in calf again and she has to calve between two set dates and that is not always easy to do.

As it happened, both Brenda and Lavenham Cherry got in calf for a suitable date which was the first bit of good luck because if they did not calve at the right time they could not go to the show, it was as simple as that. We knew we were pretty green when it came to showing cattle at this level but we did our homework and we talked to men who had been to the big shows before to get advice on how to operate and to get as much knowledge as we could on what we would do and work out what does and doesn't happen. Once they were in calf, we kept our fingers crossed; we had nine months until they calved and they needed to calve about three weeks before the Dairy Show which fell in the middle of October. As it got nearer to the show of that autumn of 1953 we talked to more people, such as our friend David Cargill, who farmed near Norwich. We were always trying to find out more and more.

Lavenham Cherry calved in good time but Brenda was hanging on. We knew she had to be calved. It was a Sunday and father and the family went to church that morning and he saw that she was in a field with her tail up about to calf, but she had to have the calf by noon that day to meet the deadline. As it turned out, she did have her calf on that last morning – just in time – and we were able to get the local vet to check and verify her, so things were beginning to happen. We had been pretty lucky with everything up to that time, so then we had to settle her down and get her on to the right food.

Father was a director of a feed firm at Catfield at the time, making cattle cake, and he had a special cake made for Brenda, which we called Brenda Nuts. We knew it had got some special stuff in it and it was good enough for the firm to sell commercially as Brenda Cake after the show, so it helped the firm as well as us. That cow cake was a big help to us to give things a little push in the right direction for Brenda at the show. The biggest problem was to make sure it did not push the cow over the top to the position where it made her ill. The digestion of the cow is what is so important and you have to think about that all of the time to get the mixture of food which works best. You really have to look after the cow if you are going to the Dairy Show and you want her to produce and we would carefully study the food we used at the Dairy Show to try to achieve that. If you get it wrong the cow gets an upset stomach and scours and the milk content goes down if the digestion system is not right. When it came to feeding a cow, George and his son Arthur, whatever else they did, were very careful to get it right and you cannot ask for better stockmanship than that.

When the time came to go down to Olympia for the 1953 Dairy Show, we had done as much as we could to be ready and Brenda and Lavenham Cherry had been prepared to the best of our ability, considering this was something new to George and me. It was a Thursday when we went to London for the show that was to last a week. During that time, the main thing for us to do was to keep the cows fit and well and eating and producing milk because they had to produce a lot of milk, as well as look good for the inspection. If they became ill, we'd had it.

Brenda and Lavenham Cherry were milked three times a day – early morning, mid-day and evening. For the milking trials there would be five milkings at the start of the show and from that five the judges could take any consecutive three but we did not know when they were doing it, or which three they would take. During the milking, the milk was carried up to a weigh point and some people stood and listened to the weighing to see who was getting a lot of milk. Brenda's milk yield was 108.1lbs in total from the three milkings that the judges selected. That was 38.0 from the first milking, 36.3 from the second and 33.8 from the third one taken by the judges.

Not only were the breeders listening to the results, but the public would watch too, so they could all see what was happening with the milkings. We were not doing that, but now I realise perhaps we should have been. My neighbour on the stall next door had been marking down the weighings, he was one of the people who had been having a look at what was happening, and after the first two or three milkings he came over to talk to us because it was clear we were getting a lot of milk. He told us that if things continued the way they were our cow was going to be wanted. I had not really appreciated that. But he was being very helpful.

'If it goes like that,' he said to me, 'feel free to ask me and my herdsman if you get any problems.'

He had been to the Dairy Show several times and was offering help, which was very kind of him. I thanked him and said I would as we were a little green. Brenda did stay up pretty high and when we were told we were going to be over 10 gallons out of the three they had taken, I was told no cow had ever won the milking trials with over 10 gallons because the butter fat often dropped because there was so much milk. Butter fat is the percentage of butter fat a cow has in its milk and there is a standard of butter fat that they had to have. When I started farming butter fat was 3.6–3.7% but we are getting 4.2% at the moment. If you get too much milk, the butter fat goes down and the milk can be a bit thin. Busting butter fat is when it falls below the minimum level and that is what could happen but it didn't with Brenda.

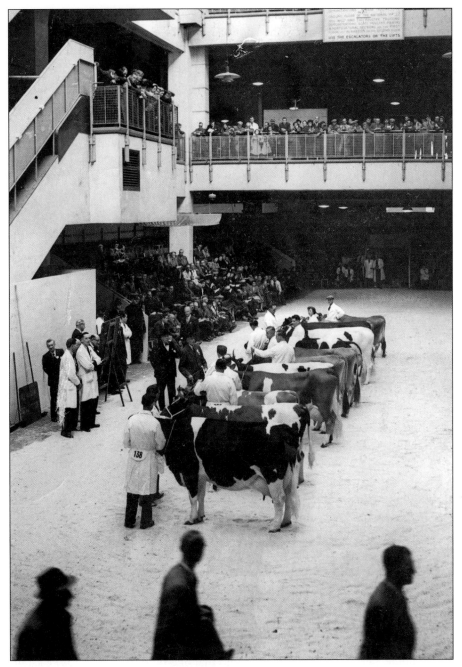

Olympia Dairy Show judging.

Her butter fat stayed at 3.8% and she got through. Perhaps with our careful way of feeding and looking after her we had done a good job, such a good job in fact that I think within the space of 24 hours Brenda had actually produced something like 13 gallons of milk. With the milking trials over, the next job was to get her freshened up and dressed up ready to show. We had a day in between for the inspection and by that stage she had not won anything. But it was possible that she might.

What we had not quite appreciated was that we should keep an eye on the cow because when we went back the next day to tidy her up and change her food she had a hard quarter; one quarter of her udder had become infected. I thought it might have been the way she was lying on the ground but it was also possible she had been given a kick in the udder and had been interfered with in the night. I have heard of that before but I had not known it myself. It was our neighbour who had noticed it, so we asked him what to do.

'If you go out the back of the show and cross the road, there is a chemist's shop,' he said. 'If you get this certain type of soap, carbolic soap, bring it back with some warm water and start to massage her bag with your hands and the soap.'

Carbolic soap was quite common at the time so we bought some and did just as he said. George and I took it in turns. We worked on her until the sweat was dripping off our brows and after a bit we asked our neighbour about how we were doing and he told us to keep on doing it. Eventually, he said, 'That will do for her.' He advised us to let her lie down and settle, not to feed her too much but give her plenty of water. We followed what he said and saw her through the rest of that day and the next morning and by that time her bag was all right. She got through her trials and there was nothing really to touch her.

Things were starting to happen for us. We knew how to show her physically as we had been to local shows such as Aylsham Show before but suddenly people were interested in us. Herdsmen and owners were coming to talk to us, asking questions and thinking that we were in with a chance. People would come to look at the cow because word was getting around that Brenda had produced a lot of milk. Sometimes they came round and looked and talked, others did not stop to talk, but mostly they were cattle people who wanted to know how she was bred and that sort of thing. Clearly, other cows had done quite well but she was against more prim cows from a show cow pedigree point of view. They were good but had not done so well in the milking trials even though they would do very well on the inspection side. From thereon we had to wait out the show until the inspection. The following day we sorted the cow out, then it was the day we had been planning for ever since we left home, perhaps ever since father said that one-off remark to me as he sat up in bed reading his newspaper.

Brenda, British Dairy Farmers Association show Class 4 No. 167, was looking pretty good on the day. We had her bag back to normal and kept her digestion right which was a factor and she was enjoying it all; she was quite happy with her situation and that was a big help. I let George take her into the ring for inspection because she was more used to him and I also thought it was his place to do that so I sat in the crowd with only a white coat on. The place was full of all sorts of people. Some had come down for a week, others just for a couple of days, to see all the updates and new machinery for the dairy farming industry and to see the best dairy cattle in the country. The man next to me was wearing a great big fur coat and was complaining about the cold and I was sitting there sweating because of all that was happening and the excitement. I would not have noticed it if he had not complained about how cold it was in Olympia. I didn't find it cold at all. I cannot really describe what I felt, I hoped we might do well but never to the extent that we did and I was so pleased for George because he had put such a lot of time in. But he always did that with cows, he knew what to do and always got it exactly right. Sat there, oblivious to the cold, I was thinking 'Is it possible?' She was a typical black and white but as cows go she was 'one helluva' cow. Some of the elite pedigree men would say she was not good enough. They might argue about that but they could

Herdsman George Clare (left) with Brenda and Gavin.

95

not complain about the amount of milk she was giving, which is really what it was all about. She won the milk production trials and in the inspection came fourth. Each breed enters and an entry from that breed becomes the Supreme Champion. Then the powers that be do their homework, put it all together and you find out how you have done. Brenda was Supreme Champion in Show and that was done there and then in the ring. I have to say, the milking trials was the key as a cow has never gone over 10 gallons and got right through the championship.

It felt good, very good. I could not believe it and it all came from that remark I made to father about some cows out there in our shed were as good as any of them in the 1952 show. It made the whole thing worthwhile to go down there and do so

Smallburgh Brenda's prize ticket.

well. It could not have gone much better, that was a special trip. There were some hiccups along the way but on the whole we were very, very lucky to get through and I was so pleased for dad because he had done so much with the cows by the time my brother and I had started beginning to work on them. I feel it was something he deserved because they were his cows. Father was there for the judging and I remember him going into the ring to receive the trophy. He was still recovering to some extent and he was not too fit but he stood it very well. It was just wonderful for father from his point of view for his lifetime's work. I knew that the Dairy Show was a big thing to win and our success was mentioned in the press at the time. A lot of people, however, had been jealous to think a popular breed of cow like Brenda could win the Dairy Show. I think that is why it was stopped eventually because people could not put up with cattle that were not pure pedigree being able to win. But I was thrilled to bits to come home and to think we had done it. Lavenham Cherry also performed well and she was third in the inspection in London in 1953 and reserve in the milking trials. We had some 60 men working on the farms at that stage and when we won the Dairy Show dad decided to have a party, so we had all 60 of them and their wives along to celebrate at

James Paterson with Brenda's show trophies and portrait.

Staff party celebrating Brenda's success at the Dairy Show.

a hall in North Walsham. After that, dad wanted us to go down to the Dairy Show every year.

Brenda went to London three times in total with George and to have a cow there three times is quite an achievement, bearing in mind you had to get her in calf at the right time on three occasions. Unfortunately, she never really repeated the success she had in 1953. The year following her initial success she burst her butter fat but in the third year she won her trials but was not good enough in the confirmation and inspection. Her beauty had gone. After that Brenda had a lot of bull calves and even a red calf that went to Dilham Manor as it was more an Ayrshire and we did sell a bull calf out of her as a non-pedigree, which made a lot of money. Brenda did very well for us, but her time eventually came. After tea on the night of 15 January 1958, George came running to the door and said he wanted a knife because 'old Brenda has blown'. She had got too much gas in her stomach and the only way to help her – to save her life – was to try and use a knife to release the pressure. George wouldn't have done it too often but he knew what he was doing and when it was performed carefully it worked and the wound to the cow would heal. But for Brenda, who was probably 10 years old by that stage, it was all too late. By the time he got back to her, she was dead.

Brenda and her rosettes, with George Clare and Gavin.

Chapter Nine

BREEDING SUCCESS

It was about the time of Brenda's success that we seriously began to go down the route of the pedigree herd. We already knew we had good cows in our herd – father did not put up with anything that was not a good cow, one that had to produce a lot of milk and have a decent udder – and it felt like the right time to establish a pedigree herd. So, it was early in my farming life that I took a herd that had not been pedigree before and gradually turned it into a pedigree herd. It was down to me to breed them and do what I felt fit with the British Friesians and Ian did the same with the Ayrshires.

In fairness, I suppose, Ian started it all off by saying he would like to go with Ayrshires. I could understand that because Ayrshire cows were the most perfect show cow, partly because of the shape of them and partly through the breeding at the time, while Friesians had other advantages. Ian always leant towards the Ayrshires anyway and father liked the Ayrshires too. Despite Ian's enthusiasm for them, I'd decided that I'd stick with the black and whites. So, having got brother Ian his pedigree Ayrshires, father and I went back to Scotland and bought some pedigree Friesians. For the first four heifers, father went to Scotland and bought from farmers that he knew well and cows he would expect to be good production cattle. In Scotland they were mostly smaller dairy farmers but they would be intensely perfectionist in their breeding and I saw all of that when I was up there at college. When it came to cows, he knew what he was looking for and he knew how to get it. That was the start of our pedigree side and that is the approach we continued if we ever needed to buy any cattle. Father would ring up Henry Brothers in Scotland – which is still there – and say he could do with two truckloads of heifers, which were about 20. He'd ask David Henry to 'look them out' and then he'd go to Scotland to have a look for himself before he bought them. More often than not, that would be in April when the Ayr Show was on. He liked to go to the show as he would meet a lot of the farmers he knew from the days before he left

Scotland to come down to farm in Norfolk. He would look at the cattle that Henry Brothers had picked out and then have them sent down to Norfolk by truck. They were usually Ayrshire in-calf heifers and then, as the Friesians became very popular because they were dual purpose with milk and meat, we had them too. In time, we started to cross Ayrshires and Friesians and it was a very good cross, it gave them more vigour as well as the dual purpose factor. Father was a real cowman and brother and I learned most of what we know about cows through him, by listening either to him or to his conversations with other people. Whatever else father was, he knew his cows and he passed it on to Ian and me and gradually we gained a lot of success from it. Cows were always a big part of our lives and if we went out on the farm with father we always ended up looking at heifers or calves somewhere or other. If we had the car and he wanted to be at the other end of the field, he would just drive it across the field to get to see his cows.

There was a herd at each of the four farms: Ian and father had Ayrshires at Dilham Manor and Dilham Hall; my black and whites were at Worstead as the Lyngate herd and father's British Friesian herd was at Church Farm, Smallburgh. Ian and father had the prefix Dilham for the Ayrshires and father's Friesians were the Smallburgh herd, which Brenda was part of. I took the prefix Lyngate for my Friesians. Worstead was already used at the Friesian Society, as it had been taken by Sir Harold Harmsworth for his herd. In the Worstead area there are hamlets such as Lyngate, Bengate and Holgate. Where I lived at the time was almost in Lyngate so I took that as my prefix for the Friesians, and for the Holstein when we switched over to them as they were introduced.

Gavin's herd was the Lyngate herd; Ian's was the Dilham herd.

My herd was inspected by the Friesian Society, or later the Holstein Society, about three times a year. The inspectors took notes and looked at the milk production, which effectively looked after itself because that was all recorded in great detail. As we developed our pedigree herd we used brochures to find out what bull semen was available and the herdsman would use that on cows. From the brochures we'd want to know if the type merit was over 3 in the Holstein Society ratings as we looked closely at that data for details such as if there is good udder composition, where the teats are and the shape of the udder. A cow's feet and legs are important as without good feet and legs, they didn't last long. You want the animal to have good composition all round and be able to walk after their food and to be able to do that for a long while. If the udder is right and she has good feet she is likely to last a lot longer. We wanted fertility and for her to breed consistently over several years as part of a herd with a good standard of animals and wearability. On average, we liked cows to have 10 calves before they were culled and some were still in quite good trim even at that stage.

While we bought some pedigree stock, we also graded up our existing herds and started breeding towards full pedigree. Brenda was ASR, which means she was inspected and was a supplementary cow. While the cows we had were not pedigrees we knew they were good cows so we started to breed them from a pedigree bull to BSR, CSR and DSR and within the four generations the offspring of that was a full pedigree. By the mid-1950s we had started to get a full pedigree herd and from that we gradually bred so that each herd became full pedigree. It was a continuous flow of breeding and as long as we used a pedigree bull we were booked down in the Holstein Society Herd Book. We were very pleased with our breeding record, so much so that eventually we placed an advert in the *Holstein Journal* which said 'we do not buy good cattle, we breed them.'

It is difficult to explain to someone who does not understand but to breed a good cow the first thing you need is a little bit of luck. Some people in Scotland used to have some wonderful show cows that were near to perfection and they would go to a lot of trouble to buy a bull calf out of the best cow they could find. Nowadays we have got AI (artificial insemination) so you can buy all sorts of bull semen but back then their man would know where there was a good herd with good cows and he would go and look at that herd and pick the best cow and say that he would have a bull calf out of that.

Father was good at picking cattle, always looking for the features that would give us an idea of how good a cow was. Sometimes it works, sometimes it doesn't work. It is a bit like buying a new car. You buy on what the paperwork says and buy on what someone tells you, then you buy it on what you think yourself and it is the same with a cow, it is your judgement based on what you know. Sometimes you can get it badly wrong, and sometimes you get it dead right and that is what the skill is in stock judging.

Originally we had British Friesians. A lot of the old British breeds had gone stale but when the British Friesians came in they were, on the whole, pretty good. They were dual purpose: you could fatten the bull calves for meat and you also got a lot of milk. Then the Holstein breed came in, which was more attractive for milk only. Holsteins grew and grew in popularity until it became the milk producing animal which was most attractive for breeders because they were profitable.

On the breeding side there are a lot of ways of being efficient and one of them is to have a calf a year with a cow. A cow is on an annual rotation and if you get her in calf so she produces the same time each year before drying up and then being in calf again that is an efficient cow. Fertility is an important factor.

Alongside building the pedigree herd, we were also improving the milking operation in the cowsheds and on the farm. Nowadays, the cow is kept free and sleeps in a stall on a bed of sand close to where there is a collecting area that herds

The cowshed built by James Paterson at Smallburgh in 1939.

them. At Worstead we extended the parlour to make it bigger with a passage right up the middle of the shed for the feeding unit. We usually milk them in batches of 32 and keep them in the same bunch which helps with the routine within the parlour system. It means a lot of cows can be handled comfortably without any interference or outside problems.

An important aspect of the operation lies in having the right stockmen and we have had very good stockmen over the years. It was often the men with big families that were attracted to dad's jobs because the first thing they wanted was continuous wages and they knew that could happen if they went to work with cows. One man in particular, who was a lorry driver before he came to us, was a fantastic stockman, mainly because he did the same thing as regular as clockwork. When you go to fetch the cows through to the parlour and they are expecting to be milked, they will know the routine and as a result be ready to be milked. If it is somebody they like and get on well with they will just drop the milk down. Cows like nothing more than routine, they are creatures of regular habit and they love to know what is happening. If you do the same thing every day without change or shouting, and if you talk to them and create a serene situation when they know they are going to be milked, they know what is going to happen and the whole operation runs so much more smoothly. A cow needs stimulation in her mind and if you can convince a cow that she is about to go to be milked, she will let her milk down and be ready and that is down to good stockmanship. It is about doing the same thing every day. They need to be relaxed and calm and even a little music may help!

There are other stockmen who took it further than that such as one of the men at Dilham who got his cows into a very good habit. When they were tied by the neck and milked in the stall there was no movement but when he let them out, he used to go up and down the middle clapping his hands and they would all do a shit. That was because he wanted the dirt to go straight into the gutter and he effectively trained his cows to do that. When people are good stockmen they get a link with the cows, they do know their cows very well and the cows know him which is maybe just as important.

We have had some wonderful cows over the years and some excellent stockmen. But what I am pleased about more than anything else is that our cows all became home bred.

Smallburgh Violet II, Lyngate Betty and Lavenham Cherry 1955.

Chapter Ten

SHOW GIRLS

I suppose it was Brenda who opened the door to my interest in showing cattle in a big way. From her marvellous success in 1953, we continued to show our cows on a regular basis right up until 2008. We went to the big shows in London and Glasgow and elsewhere across the country as well as closer to home at the Royal Norfolk Show. From 1953, following the amazing performance of Brenda, we took our cows to the London Dairy Show for a further 17 years. Not only did we think it was such a good show to attend but it also meant our cattle were being recognised nationally. We always tried to send a good team down and the timing, in the autumn, was ideal because we had more cows calving at that time of year and it gave us a bigger

Award-winning cattle; the building in the background is Holly Grove, Worstead.

selection of cows to choose from. I had a lot of enthusiasm for it but it was also wonderful to see father so excited about showing cows because producing top quality cows was at the very foundation of what he had done throughout his whole life. Father had not expected to be showing cows, it was not in his mind and was something that came about very much by accident and with us taking our chance with Brenda. But once you have had a good win like that, you get a taste for it and you want more. In the years that followed, we did a lot of showing and we had some great times out of it and in the early days I know father loved it. He really enjoyed seeing good cows and to see how good our best cows were when they were set amongst the best in the country. I think in a lot of ways that was what he deserved. The men enjoyed it too because they realised that they were very much a part of it. George Clare, the herdsman, listened carefully to father and he played his part to perfection. It was he who took Brenda to London three years running, which was no small achievement, though in hindsight, perhaps we should not have taken her back because what more could she do after her 1953 success?

Father received no end of telegrams from all sorts of sources congratulating him on his achievement with Brenda, and although a lot were from people he knew, they were also from people he had never expected to hear from. Winning the Dairy Show was something you just did not do every day and it was the show to win if you could. As a farm, our success continued at the Dairy Show and we built upon it by winning prizes every year after that for something or other. There were so many categories and we were not just showing a cow once; we were showing her for her milk, for her body and in groups for their breed and we received good prizes for that as well. More than once, we had more than one cow in the interbreed group, which was six animals from different breeds.

There was a tremendous sense of camaraderie at a Dairy Show. It was a lot of fun and a great social event for the herdsmen who would stop and talk to a lot of people and find out more about what they were doing with their cattle. We were all learning, and enjoying ourselves, but it was hard work as well. The herdsmen – and I was counted within that – all 'lived' together at the show. There was a big area with beds in it and you had to pick your bed, generally trying to find one in an area where you hoped the person next to you would not snore all night long. We didn't do much else other than what we had to do for the cattle. We were out once during the week maybe, that was about all, and it was quite funny if we got in late with the scene before us of these 200 or more beds full of people snoring away. It was a long day and there were routines to follow; we'd wake up early, in fact the whole show would rise at an early hour because stockmen were used to being about at 5am and if you were not about by then you were late. Cows are used to being milked at

5am, so we would attend to the cows and have them ready for the day. That was our priority. We would feed and milk them, bed them and make sure that they were reasonably tidy and then make a plan for the rest of the day and all that before we would go off and have breakfast in the canteen. Even the cows that were no longer involved in the show still had to be milked and properly fed and watered.

We always felt it was important to go to the Dairy Show because we became much more involved with our cows by showing them in the various classes. We often took at least three cows to the show, and more likely a team of four or five. There may be just me and the herdsman or sometimes there was a boy with us as well and on some occasions, friends would come with me too. Very quickly, showing cows got into our blood. We had fun, father enjoyed it and we were mixing with the best cows and the best breeders in the country and doing very well. Throughout the year, we were always trying to remember anything that looked right in our herd; going round and picking them out to see what stage they were at before deciding which ones to take to the big shows. We had immense pride in our herd and liked to see them look their best and do well. I always did the trimming to make sure the cows were well presented and if you got a red card (first prize) you were very pleased. It was great if you had a team because one of the most valuable prizes you could get was winning a group of three. That said a lot for your herd and on occasions we did win it. We became regulars at many of the major shows and enjoyed a lot of success. We would take our cows to the Royal Norfolk Show and Suffolk Show and from time to time the East of England Show and North West Dairy Show. We had a flit up to the Scottish Dairy Show more than once, the Highland Show and the Royal Show, though we never had as much success at the Royal Show, keeping in mind that our cows were required to always be calved, often in autumn, which meant the Royal Show in July was not the ideal time for us. However, Ian won the Royal Show with his Ayrshires as Champion and Reserve on one occasion.

The final London Dairy Show was held in 1970 and we took ten cows to that. There had been talk the previous year of it being the last one and personally I think they were wrong to finish it. The event should have continued in some shape or form. The Dairy Show was an international show and you had a lot of people come to it from across Europe and we were going to lose that. Once an event like that stops, it is difficult to bring it back. It was fiddly to do the milking trials and it cost a lot but I still think it was the most attractive event from the dairy point of view that there has ever been. I met up with a lot of people at that show, it was tremendous fun and I regretted it when it stopped.

With so many cows that year we were busy. We had Arthur Clare looking after the Lyngate herd and his father George looking after the Smallburgh cows. Sadly, father was not around to enjoy the outcome as he had died a few months earlier but it turned out to be a wonderful show from our point of view. I won it with my cows and in 1970 Lyngate Carlink II was the star. She went to the London Dairy Show four years in a row and took prizes each time: in 1967 she was second, she won the inspection in 1968, in 1969 she won the inspection and was third in production but 1970 – the final show – was her year. As the cow in first place in the inspection and third in production, she was named Supreme Champion of the London Dairy Show and was, I have to say, a remarkable cow. Cows get accustomed to being taken to the shows and they become much easier to handle each time; they get used to being clipped and fed and milked three times a day. Carlink II was well used to the routine as it was her fourth year but I had not expected her to win. I wasn't sure she was good enough but the judges thought differently. She did well with the milking and butter fat, as well as in the inspection. In the milking trials, she averaged 94.6lb at 4.62% butter fat and that was good enough for her to become the last Supreme Champion of the London Dairy Show. When the result was announced, something most unexpected happened, something that made winning very special for us indeed. Without any to do, our fellow herdsmen came into the ring and picked us up and carried me and Arthur around the ring on their shoulders, which was very sporting of them as they had not won and we had won. Emotionally that was much better than all of the rosettes you could get and it was very much an impromptu thing that happened. Most people who showed cows knew each other and their

Arthur Clare and Gavin carried on herdsmen's shoulders at Olympia in 1970.

George Clare in old age, with a model of Smallburgh Brenda.

107

cows and the other Holstein breeders must have taken note of us with Carlink II. To think that cow had gone back four years in a row, and how Arthur got that to work, was remarkable. He was a remarkable herdsman and so was his father, George, who lived until he was 90 and in the same house he had been in all his life. George died on July 1, 2005, but between them, they had been with us for a long, long time as herdsmen.

The supreme trophy of the Royal Association of British Dairy Farmers was presented to me by Princess Alexandra, who congratulated us on our success and asked questions about the cow. It was a remarkable way to end our association with the Dairy Show. At the final show, and from the 10 cows we had taken from both herds, I think we won something like 26 prizes altogether that year in milking trials, inspection, groups and progeny classes. Our cows had won on their debut at the show in 1953 with herdsman George Clare and at the last international show in 1970 with his son Arthur in charge. In dairy showing, this achievement was unique because no other father and son with separate herds had ever won the top award and no other father and son stockmen had brought them out. Arthur was fantastic; he had learned from his father George in the same way that I had learned from my father. That success had other spin-offs too. When the BBC's *Down Your Way* team was in the North Walsham district back in March 1971, I found myself interviewed as someone chosen to represent the agricultural interests of the area and I think that was down to the completion of what people regarded as a 'unique double' with the father and son teams at the Dairy Show.

Receiving the trophy from Princess Alexandra in 1970.

Besides Smallburgh Brenda and Lyngate Carlink II, there were other special cows over the years as well – Lyngate Marion, Lyngate Handsome 47, Lyngate Agnes, Lyngate Trixie7, Lyngate Countess and Lyngate Betty – who all performed consistently for us. Lyngate Marion VG86 was an exceptional cow. Her mother was bought from one of the oldest herds in Norfolk and the reason for that was simply because of her high butter fat. One of the competitions at the London Dairy Show was managed by Spillers, a popular feed merchant in those days, and the idea was to try to find the most profitable cow. What they did was to take your cow and manage it over a period of five days; they would cost the feed that the cow ate and in turn measure the amount of milk she gave as a result. Lyngate Marion did very well for us in this respect. She went down to the show twice and the first time – in 1969 – she won the Spillers Trophy and the second time she was second. That was very special. Brenda gave a lot of milk but we did not know whether she ate a lot of food to do that and whether she was economical. Winning the Spillers Trophy proved that Lyngate Marion was the most economical and profitable cow at the show.

While I remained disappointed that the London Dairy Show had disappeared, other shows came along and we were very happy to take our cows to them. We had a lot of success at the Royal Norfolk Show over the years. We were showing among people who were our friends and relations and with some success. It was always nice to win but if you didn't, you were pleased for the winners and the cups tended to go round and that was to the benefit of the show and was a huge factor to a show being successful. You were always pleased to see friends win anyway. I was honoured to receive a trophy from Princess Margaret one year at the Royal Norfolk Show when she was presenting the cups for the champion. As I received the trophy, the thing I remember most about her is those blue, blue eyes she had.

Gavin receiving the Norfolk Show championship trophy from Princess Margaret.

One of our special cows at the time was Lyngate Handsome 47 RM Excellent. She was probably the cow which won the most prizes for me over the longest period of time and was a consistent 'first-prizer,' winning 12 in all, over the seven years she went to shows as well as producing well. She took 10 lactations in ten-and-a-half years. Handsome 47 won first prize at the Royal Norfolk Show in 1975, 1976, 1978 and 1980, first prize at the Suffolk Show in 1977, she won prizes in 1979 at the first

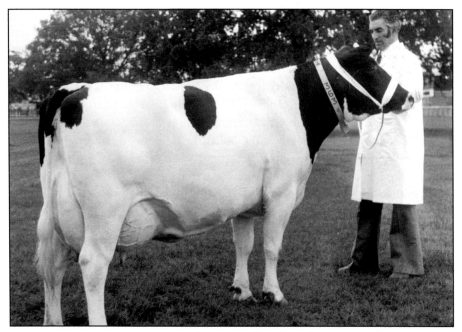

Lyngate Handsome 47 with Arthur Clare.

Highland Dairy Show and the North West Dairy Show and took a first place at the East of England Show in 1980. Handsome 47 also won the Queen's Cup at the Royal Norfolk Show in 1982, which was the top cup for different breeds, in the first year it had been given. It would be another six years before it would be held again for our breed, so we were chuffed to have won it. The cow of the original Handsome family was bought as a breeding heifer from a breeder in Scotland and Handsome 47 came from that family line. She was by a bull called Lyngate Buttermaker which was home bred. I liked that because it was another feather in our cap that she was bred with our own bull.

We did occasionally sell our cows at Norwich Cattle Market, as well as bull calves or scrap cows which were no longer used for the dairy farm. Inevitably, it came time for Handsome 47 to go but I must admit I did keep her for longer than I normally would have done. She was kept on the paddock at Holly Grove and every time the lorry came to take the scrap cows to market I'd say to Arthur, leave her until next time but eventually she had to go. The last time we won at the Royal Norfolk Show was in 2007 with a cow called Lyngate Ford Babs. She was a great success and a prize winner for me at the Royal Show. The North West Dairy Show was one of the big shows which started when the London Show stopped and it was held at Bingley Hall, Stafford, and we enjoyed going up to that one, as well as to the

Scottish Dairy Show a number of times. It was held in the Kelvin Hall in Glasgow and I was keen to go up there and we knew quite a lot of relations and friends, so it seemed a natural thing to do. It was a long way to go for the cows but when the day to set off came, the cows were transported to Norwich station and loaded into stock wagons and we'd set off for Edinburgh and from there we transferred to Glasgow. We travelled with the cattle in the wagons and it was all quite an adventure. We would arrive in Glasgow quite early in the morning and were met at the station by a cattle lorry. The cows were fed and then delivered to the Kelvin Hall at the north end of the city. It was just the same as the London Dairy Show at Olympia: you found stalls for the cows and an area for food and accoutrements and then we had to go and find a bed in a big room where I don't know how many people slept. There were a few tricks played as well. I remember coming in one night and there was a hell of a to-do going on. There were pigs in the show and someone had leant over a pen and picked one of the little piglets up and kept it quiet and then went into the area where the beds were and popped the piglet under the blanket of one of his friends. There was a great noise, the man was screaming, the pig was squealing, it was all very funny. There was a lot of leg pulling that went on.

I was still a member of Young Farmers when I went to the Scottish Dairy Show and knew a lady called Helen Kerr who was the Young Farmers organiser up there. She was middle-aged with great ability and could always see the funny side of life and we knew each other well and she would keep me up to date with what was happening and gave me a few ideas. She had a lot of knowledge and was a good organiser and she knew how to keep a friend for life. There was a Young Farmers' dance which I would go to when the Glasgow Dairy Show was on and the Young Farmers also put on a concert, which I was very impressed with and that gave me the idea that the Aylsham club could take on something similar, so for a number of years we put on a show along the same lines. I also went up to a Young Farmers' meeting in Scotland with father once to show slides about farming in Norfolk, and that was through the connections we had with Scotland.

I always remember the Scottish Dairy Show as one of the more exciting shows to go to but it was not just the big shows that we attended; we supported smaller shows too. I was a Young Farmer when the Aylsham Show first started and we were invited to help steward some of it. I, however, said I would like to show and we won the first Champion of Aylsham Show with one of our cows, even before we went to down to the London Dairy Show for the first time. We would go to all sorts of shows and meet people and it was good fun. I had always admired people who could bring cattle out and make them look beautiful.

Over the years, we have regularly supported the Aylsham Show. We are still going to it and my middle son Alexander won the 2013 championship with a second calfer. We would go to the show in some ways to train the cattle. If we had a good heifer we would take her to Aylsham Show to get her used to being washed and clipped and being led at shows. The next show we went to, probably to a bigger event, the cow would be half-

A young Ian receiving the trophy for Ayrshire Dilham Daydream at Aylsham Show.

trained and therefore ready for major shows but Aylsham has always been a good show to go to, and to show at.

I personally have had very strong connections with Aylsham Show over the years and in 1975 I was President. I remember comments being made when I was appointed along the lines that it had been noted that I was not married. As I did not have a wife, it was made clear by the committee that I would need an escort, someone special to accompany me. I think what they were saying to me was that while they wanted me as President, I had to do something about having a lady alongside me for the event. So I thought about this, did a bit of research and made a few inquiries and then went back to the committee. Obviously, what they wanted to know was whether I had a female escort lined up for the occasion. I was able to tell them 'Yes' and said, 'Will Miss UK do?' I think they were pretty surprised. I didn't actually know Miss UK personally but her name was Marilyn Ward and she came from Great Yarmouth that year. It happened that she was at an event where I was and I asked her if she would be interested in doing something she had probably not done before. So I said I would like to invite her to accompany me to the Aylsham Show in my capacity as President and present some of the trophies. And she agreed. I think the committee was all a bit shocked – in fact, so was I for that matter – and when I told them, I don't really think they believed me. But she came along and I thoroughly enjoyed the day and I think she did too. I was expecting her to go home way before the end of the show but she had no inclination to go early and she stayed for a lot longer than I expected, which was great for me and for the show.

Many of our cows that were successful over the years were first tried out at Aylsham Show and some of those wonderful cows still stand out in my mind very clearly. Smallburgh Honey was third in the inspection at the Scottish Dairy Show in 1964 and first in production in London, and Supreme Champion at the Suffolk Show in 1966. Other cows of note included Lyngate Betty, who was also one of my favourites at the time and won a lot of firsts. She was the foundation cow of the Babs family and had 12 calves in her lifetime. Lyngate Agnes was one of our best show cows. She was put on three times a day milking and fed in a way to get more milk, though as we pushed her to get more milk we needed to be able to keep her fit and well and that needed good management to help her give what she should. Agnes was ASR by a home bred bull and Ian Forsyth was the herdsman at the time. He milked 25 cows three times a day for three years, which was hard work but he was a good herdsman and got the best out of Agnes who did five lactations of over 2,000 gallons. Agnes gave nearly 19,000 gallons in her lifetime of eight lactations. She was capable and Ian knew it and a good herdsman will manage the cow to that amount of perfection. Lyngate Agnes always performed well for us. Lyngate Glen Rose, named because Arthur Clare the herdsman lived in Rose Cottage, also did well and was first at the Highland Show in 1979.

One of the great privileges and honours for me, beyond enjoying such success at the major shows, was being invited to judge. I have judged a variety of shows such as the Royal Show, the Highland Show and the Welsh Show. In 1971 I was appointed a judge of the dairy cattle inter-breed competition at the Royal Highland Show that was held in the June of that year at Ingliston near Edinburgh. As a judge, I started off by going to little shows and if people liked what they saw me doing

Gavin (LEFT) judging at the Royal Show, with David Gribbon (CENTRE).

and that I could pick the best, I was asked to do larger shows. Judging a show was an honour, not simply a pleasure, but an honour to be involved and you really set about making a good job of it.

I have been showing cows for 60 years, not so much now apart from smaller shows, but I was inspired and encouraged by father and took great pride in showing his cows alongside the best in the country, and winning many trophies, and then continuing that with cows from my own herd.

Chapter Eleven

Skiing with the
Mile-high Piper's Club

Skiing has always been a big part of my life. It was a winter holiday and a lot of fun. Funnily enough, skiing and playing the bagpipes seemed to go together for me and it was my old friend John Snook who used to be behind most of the adventures we would get up to. He was one of those people who were always great fun to be with and he seemed to make things happen.

'Bring your pipes,' he would say, as we got ourselves ready for our next ski trip, which was usually to somewhere in Switzerland, France or Austria. That usually meant packing my kilt as well as he'd normally hatch some plan or other that would lead to me playing before an audience and required me to look the part.

I first started skiing in the early 1950s when I was 21. That holiday was actually a present from my parents for my 21st birthday. It transpired that there were two other families, friends with sons the same age at the same time, so we all went skiing together. Matthew Mitchell and Billy Alston, the younger brother of John Alston who farmed at Calthorpe, were all members of Aylsham Young Farmers' Club with me. I should imagine the idea of a ski trip came from our fathers, though I wouldn't know which one it started with but they'd all meet up regularly and talk over lots of different ideas. I know Mr Mitchell went to church in Norwich with father and Jim Alston, who was a real livewire of a Scot, was on one of the farmer's committees so they all knew each other. We were all interested in skiing and very keen but none of us knew anything about it. We had no idea what we were talking about or what to expect and as a result I suppose we didn't really prepare very well at all for a trip at a time when they were still using wooden skis, which I do recall weren't that strong.

That first trip was to Switzerland, through Thomas Cook tours, and we were in a group of people on a chartered plane. It was quite a long trip and by the time we arrived at the hotel, we were late for the meal. However, none of us were prepared for the sight which greeted us when we walked into the dining room. About a third of the people sitting at the tables had their heads bound up, with arms in slings and injured legs. It looked quite a sight. They were already having their meal by the time we sat down and as we joined them our faces just got longer and longer. We were about half way through the meal when all of a sudden they burst out laughing. It was a joke, a very good one, but we hadn't appreciated that because some of them had made their injuries look very real, even using tomato sauce as blood!

We were there for a fortnight at what was pretty much a beginners' resort. There wasn't actually that many of us but the next day, we were up and all ready to head off to the ski equipment shop to collect our skis and hire our boots. We ambled around, learning to walk in them and get used to wearing ski boots. We hadn't been allocated our instructor by that stage but we were keen, so we got ourselves up onto the nursery slopes and gave it a go. There was the three of us from Norfolk, plus six others, and as we started to walk about some of us soon became quite nimble and ventured up the hill to try to get a run down. We weren't that successful and fell over a few times because we hadn't met our instructor so we didn't really know what we were doing. We had no idea how to control ourselves or even turn so it was no surprise that with an electricity pole in the middle of the hill there was going to be a mishap. That saw one chap finish up with his legs either side of it but thankfully he didn't hurt himself too badly.

From there, we joined a ski school where we learned how to control our skis. My first thought was that this was going to be a hell of a job to do well, but we started with our lessons and gradually got an idea of how to start to ski. The first day, however, wasn't without incident. I started to turn but as I lifted my skis I overbalanced and went over and somehow I managed to break one of my wooden skis. The instructor was quite calm about it and said it was no problem, even though we were halfway up the mountain. He gave me one of his skis and then he skied down on one ski. That was quite a demonstration from our instructor on the first day of my introduction to skiing.

We didn't progress that quickly in the first week, but gradually got to know how to control our skis and our speed as well and once you can control your speed everything seems to go a lot better, or at least it felt as though it did. I enjoyed my first ski holiday but I was really quite pleased to go home in one piece; I always felt that way after every ski holiday I went on. I couldn't wait to get back to the slopes either. Many a time I thought that we should be going for three weeks at a time or have another fortnight on the slopes in the same year so we could really improve our skiing but never managed to do that, mainly because there was always a lot to do back home on the farm. The weather was always better in the mountains if you left it later in the season but the same applied on the farm so when the spring came we had to get on with it and I had to be there. But the men, Arthur Clare and George Goodwin who was my foreman at Worstead, always said to me 'Go away and enjoy yourself, we will look after things here.' And they always did. When I got back I used to tell them about it and how exciting it was but also how I was pleased I hadn't broken anything.

In those early days there were up to six of us who went out skiing together, but as people got married they dropped out. One of the chaps I went with was Peter Day, a sales merchant for farming machinery. I was at school with him and we used to meet up for a drink at the Trowel and Hammer on Newmarket Road in Norwich. We were in there one night when he invited me to go skiing with him and a friend from Ipswich that he had skied with before. I couldn't go as I was doing something. I was probably at a dairy show or something similar. He talked to me about what he and his friend – John Snook – got up to and that it was a laugh from beginning to end. But he suggested that we go the following year, which we did, and it was, as he said, a laugh a minute. That was how I met Snooky. He didn't force it upon you but sometimes he would set something up which we had no idea was going to happen, or often he would say something funny or pull someone else's leg and make us all laugh. As the ski trips went by, rarely did we go without taking my bagpipes with me and it was usually my friend John Snook from Ipswich who was at the root of it. He had a great sense of fun and I suppose he was my 'manager' at the time. Snooky had also walked down the aisle but his wife had a quiet word with me and said, 'Whatever you do, you must still take John skiing with you as he enjoys it so much. I would be in the doghouse if you did not take him.' So despite getting married, he never dropped out of the ski trips. John and I always had great fun together; he could make fun out of very little I suppose and it was his character that took us into a lot of funny situations.

As well as having fun, our skiing improved. We would go up the drag lifts and gradually got used to them. We had a tumble or two but once the instructor takes over you are away and from there we learned a bit more every year. On one holiday we discovered our instructor was sitting at another table in our hotel one morning having his breakfast. It turned out that he had married the daughter of the hotelier, so that night when we got back to base we asked him to have a drink with us, which he enjoyed. From then on we got on very well with him. He said to us on one of the days, maybe it was a dirty old morning and there weren't many people on the slopes, that we should go out with him. He said to the three of us, 'I want you to follow me right close, close enough that you think you are going to hit me, and do exactly what I do.' So we did. We went over a little bump and down the slope and were right up with him all the way, only a metre behind his skis, so we all did exactly the same thing and I felt that was the day that I really learned to handle my skis. It felt tremendous and before long we were good enough to do black runs and off-piste skiing in the powder.

Snooky often used to book our ski holidays and on some occasions he made a better job of it than others. There was the time he booked us into a hotel that can only be described as a bunk house, where there were no frills. We had a bed but there was no wardrobe to hang our clothes in and we lived out of the suitcase all holiday. When we wanted to wash we had to go to a trough where there was a continuous flow of warm water which everybody had to shave in. That was the cheapest ski trip I ever had and I was a little perturbed about how skimpy we had been in the way we spent our money. It was not very comfortable. We started in a big room with about 10 beds and one poor devil came with a cold and he spread it around us all one at a time so he was not popular and as the rest of us caught it, we were not very popular either. I was complaining about this to John when he disappeared for a while. When he came back he said he had got things sorted out.

'I've just been to the best hotel in Zermatt and had a chat with the manager,' he told me. 'I asked him if he was aware that a very famous piper from Norfolk in England was staying in the town. I told you were prepared to come along and pipe in his guests for dinner each night if in return he would give us a meal. And if he had a spare room we would like that as well.'

That sounded quite appealing but I suggested to Snooky that he was expecting a lot. However, I had my instructions and we had to be there ready for when the diners wanted to go in at 8pm for their dinner. On the dot, I opened up with the pipes and piped all the

The 'best hotel in Zermatt'.

hotel manager's guests in to dinner. He was delighted and said that we should stay for the meal in return. That all went very well and we had a lovely meal but there was no bed and breakfast for us, which is what we really wanted. So, after it was all over it was back to the bunk house and the shaving trough. But we had a great laugh out of it.

On one such occasion John had got it into his head that I should play the pipes,

I think it would have been back in Switzerland, I needed to get them ready for playing. So, I went well out of the way and got behind a big shed and started tuning the pipes. After I'd finished tuning up, I heard what I thought was a clapping sound and that maybe there was someone about who had liked what they heard. I had a look around and then realised there wasn't anybody there . . . apart from the shed full of cows. The sound of the pipes had excited them and all the cows were making dung. So rather than someone clapping, the sound I heard was effectively a 'round of applause' from the cows in the shed.

We took part in talent contests too and did well. At one of the hotels we had visited in Austria I won jointly with a girl singer and had another good meal for nothing. We soon discovered that if you wanted to have fun, there was always great potential with the pipes and we always got a good reception. It was John who had entered me for the competition to play but the girl we tied with for first place was a very good singer. I usually played marches, or slow marches in particular, and I always wore my kilt, which meant taking more clothes than normal for a skiing holiday.

There were other ways we had a laugh too. One of the places we stayed in Austria was an old wooden building where the walls were thin. On a typical day we'd finish skiing at about 4pm and would unwind, have a drink and some après ski and then go back to the hotel and hop into bed and have some sleep before getting up for a meal and be ready to go out for the night. We never wanted to miss any of the nightlife. One time we were in our beds in this big hotel, which was the type of building where you could hear things through the walls. Suddenly, we heard this voice boom out from our neighbour's room.

'Woah Nelly, you're one helluva woman.'

Well, we didn't really know who said that but when we got up and went out John laughed and suggested that the owner of the voice was standing nearby in a group.

'I'm sure it's the fella in that group, I'm certain it's one of those,' he said.

He told us to keep our eyes open as he went over and that he'd say something that would raise his ears. John was just out of their view and while he was looking the other way, he said 'You're one helluva woman, Nelly.' Well, this chap jerked up and looked around and when Snooky sidled back over to us, he said 'Told you, that's him' and he was right.

We had some great adventures too and some wonderful opportunities that came our way. When we were in St Moritz we met up with a chap who was going to do the bobsleigh run – the Cresta Run – and asked us if we wanted to come with him. He went down on what was no more than a little sledge, laid on his belly with his nose out in front and his legs hanging over the back to steer it with. Then he asked us if we would like to have a run down the course. You could go from the middle station and if you went too fast all that would happen was that you would shoot off the track and end up in a pile of snow, so there was nothing to worry about. John decided he wasn't going to have a go, it looked too frightening, but I said I'd have a go. It was too good an opportunity to miss, I was used to sledging and knew roughly how to steer it with my legs. So before I knew it, this man was putting the gear on me and getting me ready to go. I had the headgear, a helmet on, and great big gloves, and my ski boots to which he attached a set of spikes. They were strapped to my toes and were what I was to use to stop the sledge if I wanted to. I soon discovered how to control and steer the sledge with my feet as I set off from the middle station. Beginners weren't allowed to go right from the top because they would get such a speed up and if they weren't used to it that would be dangerous. In the end, I did three runs from the middle station; I didn't come out of the track at all and was pleased with that. At the start of the run it was cold but by the time you got to the bottom, in less than a minute, you were sweating hot. I was in my ski suit and I was soaking wet. It just showed how much you sweated in such a short space of time doing that run. From my point of view, I thought I was going fast but when you saw the people going from the top, you realised how much faster they were going. I did see one chap come off. He just flew off the track, him and his sledge and landed in a drift of snow. I must say, doing the Cresta run was one of the biggest thrills of my life. I have had things that have excited me but nothing quite like that did.

We often used to fly from London for our skiing trips, usually overnight because it was cheaper. There was a Scottish airline we used back then called Caledonian Airways. On one of our flights we thought we would have a bit of fun so I said to the stewardess walking up and down the aisle that I was somewhat disappointed that, as a Scottish airline, there was not much of a tartan theme.

'It's not living up to its reputation as Scottish,' I pointed out.

She said she hadn't had anyone comment on that before but seemed interested so I asked her if she had ever had a piper walking up and down among the passengers. She said no.

'Would you like a piper walking up and down the aisles? If you like, I'll get my bagpipes out, they are only under my seat, and I can play for you and the passengers,' I told her.

She was fine with the idea but said she'd better warn the pilot first. He was over the moon and thought it was a great idea, so out came my pipes and before long I was marching up and down the aisle playing the bagpipes at 30,000 feet. Not so long after, the pilot asked to see me on the flight deck so I went forward to talk to them and told them they were missing a trick being a Scottish airline without anything Scottish, but they were pleased to have me playing the pipes on board.

I even played the pipes at the airport. Once when we arrived back in London the porters were on strike so there was nobody to take the bags from the aircraft and get them to the returning passengers. It appeared it was going to be a long wait before the flight people were going to be able to bring them to us in the airport. We were instructed to go up to a reception on an elevator where we saw other people who had been on the plane with us and told to wait there for our luggage. We hadn't been there very long before one chap, who had brought his guitar with him, started playing. It sounded lovely. People were singing along and then John turned to me and said he'd had an idea.

'Why don't you just quietly take your pipes and go down again and when I give you a wave, you come up the elevator and start playing?' he suggested. So I did that and I came right up to the top playing the bagpipes. John said to me later that he had a word with the guitar player and asked him if he would mind stopping playing for a few moments as I came up from the lower level and he was happy to do that. That was typical of Snooky, he always had a plan.

Snooky and I were going skiing every year together and we just clicked. We got on so well together but were from different ways of life; he was an auctioneer, he sold bric-a-brac, antiques and all sorts of things as well as property. He was just a one-off, I cannot explain, but we just had a lot of fun together. Going away at that time of year suited him and it suited me as well because of the farming calendar, the only thing we didn't want to get out of skiing was a gammy leg. There were so many other things going on that were good fun, such as cattle shows or sales, but they were not holidays. Skiing was something we enjoyed doing very much and after that first year I went skiing every year after for the next 30 years and eventually I bought my own boots as I got better. I also bought a pair of skis, metal ones, which were much better and shorter than the wooden ones and easier to manage. There is no doubt, I had a great time skiing. Snooky and I had so much fun and by the time we finished we were competent. I was happy, as I had got to be as good as I wanted to be on the slopes.

Chapter Twelve

WORSTEAD FESTIVAL

The Church of St Mary the Virgin has stood proudly in the centre of Worstead for many centuries. It was, like many Norfolk churches, built on the wealth of the wool and cloth trade and there are few places more famous than Worstead for cloth. As children, we had sat in the box pews of the church but we were from Scotland and father and mother were Presbyterian so we didn't go to the local church all of the time. As a family we sometimes went to the Presbyterian Church in Norwich, which was near the Theatre Royal. It was demolished during World War Two when it suffered a direct hit by a bomb but a new Presbyterian Church was built in the years after the war near the Roman Catholic Cathedral and father would often attend that. But Worstead church had always been there for me as a landmark in the village and in my life, standing tall and solid opposite Manor Farm House. I saw it virtually every day of my life. The tower was more than 100 feet high and we regarded it as solid, sturdy and safe. But, as it turned out, that wasn't the case and during the early 1960s it was discovered that there were two big cracks in the walls of the tower. I am not heavily religious but I am conscious of the fact that I live and make my living out of farming in the parish of Worstead and I was of the view that just because I am not going to the church on a regular basis, I cannot ignore it. When it became apparent how serious the situation was with the tower, some villagers and churchgoers joined together to see what they could do about it. I was approached by the then vicar, the Reverend Joscelyn Fellowes-Brown, who asked if I would be prepared to join the Church of St Mary Restoration Committee and that is what I did. In the olden days the estate, or owner of the estate, would be expected to support a project such as this and we felt that now, as owners of the Worstead Estate, we had a responsibility in this respect. If the estate had still been owned by the Harmsworth or Rous families, they would have been expected to support the church. I believe that one of the conditions of renting a house on the estate would have been that the occupants went to the church regularly. Now, that

Worstead church tower under repair.

is part of old England tradition poking its head up. But I did think that when the problem with the church arose, and as we were farming in the village, we should be part of the move to help out and that is what started me off in that direction. There were also other keen members of the church involved, in particular Sir Edmund Neville from Sloley, who was a great help because he was interested and was also on the committee of the Norfolk Historic Churches Trust and he already had great knowledge on such things as repairing churches.

Until we held a proper investigation of the structure of the church we did not realise how dangerous things were getting, or how much it would cost to put right. The findings came as quite a shock to us all. It emerged that there was a split in two walls of the church tower on the south side – wide enough that a man could crawl through. Now that is a big hole. I did go up there to the top of the church to look at it myself and it was a hole big enough that I could have got through it. Later, when measurements were taken it emerged that one of the cracks was 40 feet long and 18 inches wide in one place. That was too far for safety's sake but until that was examined in detail we did not know that. Something had to be done but how that would happen and who would do it was the big question. The church had a congregation at the time and people who were used to dealing with regular Sunday events but that was not the same as restoring the church so they had to look outside of the church community to see who could help them. I still do not think we make enough of the history of Worstead but that is the sort of thing that comes in waves; some people in the village will get excited about it for a period of time and then you get nobody in the village who wants to do anything. But the village, which was mentioned in the Domesday Book, was a sleeping giant when it came to history, not only in Worstead but in Norfolk and indeed the woollen industry. It was talked about but nothing was really done.

The idea was that we needed to form some kind of organisation that could tackle this issue and could help save our village church from falling down. We also needed to raise a lot of money to put the problem right. Some £36,000 was needed, which was a big amount back then. We started to get people involved; some from the village, some from outside. We started in a small way to begin with. First of all, we put a donation box in all of the cottages of the village, some called it a swear box, to start the fund-raising. During the winter of 1965–66, bingo and whist drives were held and brought in some cash but it was clear it would take too long to raise the necessary amount that way. With Worstead having such a history through its connection with the cloth trade, we wrote to every business we could find in England that used the word 'worsted' in helping sell their products, such as worsted suits and worsted cloth, which was common at that time as worsted cloth was well known for its wearability. It was worth writing the letters, and a good idea, but we as a restoration committee were left very disappointed with the replies. Some businesses did not bother in replying but those that did reply would say they had already spent all the money allocated for this year for their charities.

We weren't going to be put off and sat down and started to think again how we could help raise money, so we searched everybody's minds to try to find something we could do ourselves within the village. One of the people came up with the idea of a village show and call it an 'open village' event where visitors would come in from outside and walk around gardens and have a cup of tea and enjoy being in the sunshine. The 'open village' idea was the initial thought and once set, we started to think about adding things like stalls in the square and other things that a village could put on for people to take part in. This was the first seeds of an idea that turned into the Worstead Festival.

It was 1966, the year of the World Cup in England, and we were getting more offers of ideas and people coming forward to make them happen. The Women's Institute offered to do the catering in the old village hall. The main events were meant to be in the village square with visitors invited to walk around the church which would have displays of flowers and stalls as well. There were a number of people who were used to working for the church, so they were happy to help – people like Mrs Chapman who offered to run the stalls. She was one of the people who stuck to doing something and was also good at encouraging other people to help her. Her father-in-law, Dan Chapman, worked for me so I knew the family very well. When I was young and lived at the Manor House before the war, Old Dan used to be the horseman and he would lock up the barn at night and bring the keys back to the rack on the back door. We would be sitting there and see him in the light, looking through the back door. It would open and there would be the jangle of keys and Dan had this trick where he would raise his hat by raising his eyebrows. It always made us laugh.

We started to make positive plans. The open day was the main idea we had and was suggested by a lady on the committee. We were told to think about it some more and make bigger plans to bring back to the committee. Not everybody, however, was that enthusiastic or positive. One man on the committee felt we'd never get people in Worstead to do an event like that. That put us off a little bit because he was a man who had been in the village all his life and knew the people well.

I began to think it was pretty uninteresting to just call it an open day, the idea being that people open their houses and sell things and have people walk around their gardens. They should also look at visitors bringing something to sell – better still, bring and buy. One day, I was listening to the wireless where they were talking about the King's Lynn Festival. It was a regional festival but it was the name 'festival' that I wanted to get established rather than just an open day and get across the idea that we were celebrating something rather than just raising money. By this time I had begun to make bigger plans myself and that involved using the labour of the farm over what was the old Bank Holiday weekend. When the committee decided to make it that weekend, we agreed to start with the two days of Saturday and Sunday but I felt we should think about starting it on a Friday because if we wanted the crowds to come on that Saturday and Sunday we really wanted to be ready before that, so we agreed we would go on the Friday as well and make it a three-day event.

I started to think about us using the farm for some of the activities so we came up with the idea to open the farmyard with calves and sheep and other animals. It was an idea that did go very well but there was a lot involved in getting the place ready for visitors in terms of littering and feeding the animals and also ensuring it was safe for people to walk around. I suppose from the point of view of the village, Manor Farmyard being open was a big step. We had the cattle to move and we then offered some of the space to people from outside who brought all sorts of peculiar animals. We also had Highland Cattle from my uncle Rob from Witton with their great big horns, and he brought them, and then dressed to match by wearing his

Sheep in Worstead churchyard.

kilt. But we had to be careful with their horns and that they didn't swing round and catch someone. The farmyard was another aspect where we had to think about the safety side of things but it was great to allow children to stroke the calves' nose, something they might not have done before. Sometimes we had a man with food for the sheep and lambs. We had the Norfolk breed of sheep that was the breed that started the Worstead weaving industry off as they produced the wool that was woven into worsted cloth. Eventually, we'd have them in the churchyard over the festival weekend. We had some fun with the festival; one year we dyed three sheep red, white and blue and said we were breeding sheep that did not need to be dyed a colour as they were already coloured.

We advertised stalls for people to hire and we would always look out for people who were making something unusual or special such as jewellery. If they made it themselves we liked that and in particular if they were making something different and not something that you could just buy in a shop, something that they had invented or created from wood, for example, better still. There were lots of stalls and stands and there were shopkeepers selling vegetables. The whole thing came from the enthusiasm of the village as a whole. What came out of it was tremendous. People did not just help, they put themselves out in a big way – they suddenly realised this was something that could work and could help look after their church. There were people coming from all over Norfolk with animals that they used to show and then they started bringing small items that went with their trade and they had stalls. We also invited 10 charities and offered them a site for nothing. They used to make a lot of money from the festival, several thousands of pounds, and that to some extent helped them. They were not always invited back the next year because we wanted to give other charities a chance; we did do things that were of benefit to a lot of organisations outside Worstead as well as raising money for the church. We also talked to the police about how we should manage car parking and we decided the farm grass fields were the place, and it has been ever since. The police were concerned about two things – one was the traffic and how we were going to handle the traffic and the other was drink. They were very good but we approached them because we were concerned about keeping within the law and making sure that other people did, and the police seemed happy with that.

The first festival took place on the weekend of 29, 30 and 31 July 1966. It was the weekend of the World Cup Final and England were playing West Germany at Wembley Stadium. I can remember sitting in my lounge and watching some of the World Cup Final as people walked by to the festival. The help was all in place, the WI did the food and the *Eastern Daily Press* also decided to help us with advertising, provided they could be the main sponsor of the event. We all knew what we had to do and why we were doing it; we were trying to raise money to spend on the church, so we were going to work hard to do that. We knew we needed a lot of money for the church – £36,000 is what we were told it would take to do the job, though what happened was that the job got bigger and bigger and bigger.

An early Worstead Festival: with Snowy Gleave and Gavin's Bentley.

Our car parking worked well and we directed the cars to the grass fields, which I supplied (and still do). We directed them in such a way that they did not pass through the centre of the village at all and when they were at the parking area they were close to the things that were going on. For anything further away, there were signs to point visitors in the right direction around the village. They would generally go through the farmyard first and on from there into the centre of the village and the church. There were a lot of stalls in the square and more in the churchyard and the flowers looked marvellous inside the church.

We were successful. The event went well and because of what we achieved in the first year, people talked about it. We had no way of knowing how many people came along to that first Worstead Festival because we were selling tickets on the gate or door to get into the farmyard or the church. It was, I remember, very cheap because while we wanted to raise money we did not want to sting people with big families. Admission to each property was one shilling (5p) or a book of tickets cost ten shillings (50p). We also tried to attract holidaymakers as well. What we have learned over the years is that Worstead people are very interested in the festival; some people still come every year, even though they may have left the village, and they bring their families and children or now their grandchildren back to visit. It went very well and we were relieved when it was over. The first festival raised £1,800 and ended with a service in the church.

We had put on the festival making the most of what the village had and without using a playing field, because, actually we didn't have one in Worstead. It was at that point, in the mid to late 1960s, that I started to think that Worstead needed a playing field. Dilham had one and that was there because of a landowner who, in the past, had made land available. Worstead did have a field where they played football, which was a grass field with a wooden hut on it for use as a changing room but that was not really good enough because there was not enough space. I started to look at the map of the village and began to think about how the village would be much better off with a playing field. There would be more room for the festival and if there was something permanent it should be near the centre of the village, near the pub and the church. The nearest bit of land was allotments that the estate let to people who wanted some additional garden space and that was next to the White Lady pub, which had two acres of land. It was pretty clear that was where the playing field should be but two acres was not enough. (The White Lady pub used to be called the New Inn at one stage but changed its name more recently to reflect one of the great tales of the village which suggests that a ghost of a white lady appears at midnight on Christmas Eve in St Mary's Church.)

When I watched Norwich City in the past, I used to sit next to a director of the brewery which owned the pub at the time, and I asked if there was a chance we could buy the two acres of land that ran alongside the church because we were looking to make a playing field for the village of Worstead. He knew the land near the pub was in an ideal position so he said he would think about it. He eventually came back to me and said he'd sell it, so I bought it from him and took out the hedges in between and added the other acres from my field at the back so that made space for about a five-acre site for a playing field. We levelled it, drained it and created a football pitch and made it available to the village. I didn't give it to the village at the time but instead said they could have the playing field to use for a peppercorn rent of £1 a year. I was asked why I didn't just give it to the village. But my solicitor advised me to go down the peppercorn rent route as he suggested that if I gave the land to the village, they might later not allow me to have a say in what that land is used for. I have seen playing fields that were not looked after properly, where rough grass has grown, and I did not want to see that happen in Worstead. But in Worstead, the playing field is looked after very well. I hope they continue to appreciate it. Another reason why I keep the site is to ensure that it is not sold off and used to build houses on. However, the land that the village hall was later built on had to be transferred to the village before it could be built so they could get a grant. I felt that one of the things that I could do for Worstead was to supply the playing field and it made a big difference to the village. I also began to think the playing field was in the logical place. The school might have said why not put it near the school as they could have used it but the school was not near the pub or the village and the church and there is no guarantee that the school will be there forever.

After the first year of the festival there was money to put into the restoration committee kitty, which was more or less used straightaway on the church. They were ready to start work by that time, and needed to, because we were all worried about whether the side would fall out of the tower. If that happened, it would have been an even bigger, and much more expensive, job. That was at the beginning of the festival and the start was, in a way, somewhat haphazard but it took shape and began to be successful and we all wanted to change and improve things in the village where we could. We did get more organised as we went along and we divided into two committees; the restoration committee and a committee to run the festival. I became chairman of the festival committee and that was a natural step because so much of what was needed for the festival was connected with the farm. It was a big commitment for us as well, because we could not start our harvest until after the festival.

For the second year of the festival, we had an enormous piece of luck and something that made a huge difference and it could not have come from a higher source: Queen Elizabeth, the Queen Mother herself. Someone on our festival committee had connections and managed to set it up for the Queen Mother to offer a half set of china, which was called Roses china, as a raffle prize. This attracted a huge amount of publicity and gave us a great deal of confidence too, knowing that somebody like the Queen Mother would do something like that for us. The Queen Mother's tea set stimulated both committees and I do not think even she would realise how big an effect that would have on our festival. Later, when I met her when she opened the village hall, I was able to thank her for that. The raffle raised £600 and was televised and brought in a lot of much-needed publicity.

We had another successful year with the second Worstead Festival and, given that boost by the Queen Mother, we were determined to keep going. We wanted to keep growing and for more people to come, though we also wanted them to have a good value day out. We didn't want them to think they were being stung for money, we wanted them to feel that the Worstead Festival was an event worth their while coming to see. We also tried to encourage a lot of younger people to come as well. The festival just kept creeping forward from thereon; it got bigger and bigger and we got better at handling it. Those joining the committee for the first time perhaps felt a bit at sea with what to do but we kept going. The one thing about Worstead

Festival that we were always so lucky with was the weather. We possibly had two festivals with showers or rain but we had so little rain overall. Even when we did have a wet time it would seem to stop at the right moment and the sun would shine. We would say it was 'Worstead Festival weather' and it will not rain. With festivals where we did have rain, it often didn't start to rain until 6pm on the last day when everybody was finishing. The weather was always so kind to us.

There were lots of great stories that came out of the Worstead Festival and we all had a lot of fun doing it. One of the funniest was with Bob Spanton, who was one of the traders in the village and he delivered coal and firewood round the cottages

Festival characters: Bob Spanton, Dan Chapman, Gordon Mosley.

and visited virtually everybody in the village for many years. He knew most people, and that was his secret. He managed to get an organ grinder from somewhere and would rattle out a melodic tune and then he started to dress up like an old fortune teller woman and began to read people's palms. No-one really knew who 'the fortune teller' was and Bob was marvellous at it. There were a lot of people who went up to him to have their palm read, people he knew extremely well but they did not know him in his disguise. With some of the people, he knew so much about them as he was always in their homes. He probably knew their whole life story. It was all good fun and part of entering into the spirit of the festival. At one stage we said we thought we should create a traditional atmosphere in Worstead by dressing up in the style of people from an old Norfolk village and some people did this very well indeed and it worked for quite a while. Of course, as chairman of the committee, I couldn't just talk about it I had to dress up myself. So, I put on a top hat and rode a penny-farthing bicycle through the village. Even that dropped on my plate. I happened to mention to someone I knew that I wanted a penny-farthing and because we were doing the festival, people always tried to do something for us. This man in Smallburgh had one but was moving to London, so he let me have his

Gavin on his penny-farthing.

penny-farthing. It is hard to get on a penny-farthing and even harder to get off but I somehow managed it. I still have it even now.

At one stage I also bought a 1926 Bentley for the festival from a man in Sussex. Snowy Gleave and I went down to look at it and we decided to buy it. The garage man in Sussex brought it up to Norwich and Snowy and I picked it up from there and we used it for rides at the festival. I had three old cars at one stage; an old Austin and Humber Super Snipe as well as the Bentley and later I sold them at an old car sale at Duxford. Funnily enough the next time I saw the Bentley was in a magazine in Australia. I also bought an old horse-drawn hearse, which was on sale at the Suffolk Show and was in magnificent condition. We had an antique roundabout for the Worstead Festival one year, which I later sold at an auction, and I also bought a model steam engine which we put on display and had being driven by an electric motor to show how it worked.

Snowy Gleave with James Paterson and the 1926 Bentley.

One of the most unusual, but also very practical, items I laid my hands on for the Worstead Festival was an old Gypsy caravan. It was in a scrapyard on the other side of Norwich when I first saw it. There was a leak in the roof and a hole in the floor. Overall, it was in pretty bad shape and a sad sight all around. There was a carpenter who worked for me at the time called Billy Cooper. He had been on the estate as the repair man for the cottages for many years before we bought the estate, so we got him with the estate but his health was not too good. He would keep smoking and was always coughing. One day Billy came riding up on his bike, he was wheezing and coughing as he came into the carpenter's shop where I'd had the caravan brought back to. I asked Billy if he could repair it. I was looking for an inside job for him for the winter, and to me this seemed ideal for him. He was very keen and said he'd be interested in doing that as a job so he spent the winter doing it up. He repaired the roof and floor and started to look at the paintwork. I wanted it to look good but I was also interested to find out a bit more about it. I didn't know who the original owner was but asked around and eventually found they were horse dealers and from that I had a rough idea who they were. One day I saw one of their vehicles outside the pub at Worstead, so I went into the bar and said to the man leant against it, 'Have you got 10 minutes to spare? I've got something I would like to show you.'

I took him into the barn where the caravan was completely finished and painted up; it looked a marvellous sight. Billy was a good carpenter and did the job very well indeed and had also done some investigating to find out the correct colour scheme. The man I'd found at the bar just stood there with his mouth open. It was his father's old caravan.

'The last time I saw it, it was a wreck,' he said to me. I told him the story about Billy repairing it and he began to tell me a little bit about the history to it and how it found its way into a scrapyard. He said he still had a stove that belonged to that caravan but was never used and he offered to sell it to me so I went off to his house and it was there on the hearth. There was also a brass rail that belonged to the caravan that was being used to stop logs rolling on to the floor, which he asked if I also wanted to buy, so I ended up buying two more of the original pieces of the caravan that we were missing.

'My father should have been burned in that when he died but that didn't happen,' he said. 'We didn't know what to do with it, so it must have eventually ended up in the scrapyard.'

He was very pleased to see it done up and restored to its former glory and we put that caravan to good use that summer at the next festival. It became the festival's moveable office for the secretary and if it wasn't in the right place, we just moved it but in most of the programmes from then on the caravan was listed as being in the main square.

There was always so much going on at the festival and we detailed most of it in the programmes for the event. There were demonstrations of weaving, spinning and lace-making by the St Mary's Worstead Guild of Weavers, Spinners and Dyers, while activities in the village square included a ride on a steam wagon and farm wagon. Various other displays were being held in people's houses and in the farmyard were animals and their young while the village hall hosted the Annual Festival Horticultural Show. That was something Dan Chapman had started. Most years, the programme had notes on the history of Worstead and also about people who had contributed to the festival over the years. Looking through the 1989 programme, someone had written about young Dan. He had been struck down with polio in his youth but trained as a horticulturist. He was involved with the Worstead Festival from the first year, albeit in a small way when he had a stall under the stairs in the Manor House. The following year he suggested that a horticultural show should form part of the festival. It was a good idea, and he was asked to organise it, which he did successfully for the following 19 years until interest waned and it was no longer held but it didn't stop Dan continuing to play a part in the Church's contribution to the festival.

*Worstead Festival
programmes.*

The programme listed seemingly endless activities. There was a Punch and Judy Show on the paddock, swimming advertised in the Holly Grove pool, a rifle range and sideshows in the marquee and in Holly Grove Barn things such as pottery demonstrations and paintings were taking place. There was the annual Festival Concert on the Saturday night, a country and western dance, the Worstead 5K run, a cock crowing competition, the Starting Handle Club bringing old tractors, vehicles and engines, and so many other interesting attractions. Other ideas included Miss Worstead Competitions, Flamenco and Highland dancers, dog

*The restored Gypsy caravan with Bill
Nash and Bishop Maurice Wood.*

shows, and dwile flonking which is an old Norfolk game which involves two teams with one dancing around the other while attempting to avoid a beer-soaked dwile – or cloth – thrown by the non-dancing team. The programmes were important in detailing all the events that were on over the three days and giving an idea of how much the festival has raised. The 1974 Festival, for example, raised £3,434 and enabled the urgent restoration work to be completed and by the late 1970s, the festival had raised enough money to start a phased restoration of the church, which effectively secured its future.

If you look at the 1977 programme – which was the 12th Worstead Festival – we had a special insignia on the front for the Queen's Silver Jubilee. The festival took place over the weekend of 29, 30 and 31 July and as festival chairman I'd write a piece in the programme, reminding people what the festival was about. My message in 1977 was to look back and then focus on the present and the future. I wrote: 'In 1966 it became quite obvious that the centrepiece of our village, the kernel of its history – the Church of St Mary – was in peril. Thus a small band of people mindful

of tradition and retention of heritage decided to take action. The plan of the Village Festival evolved with the idea that this small community should 'think big'. The idea frightened some but was an added spur to others.'

By 1977, as festival chairman, I had recorded that £83,000 had been raised so far and I added 'the "think big" has been proved successful to such a degree that it has now been possible to give limited assistance to associations beyond the parish who have tried, as we did, to help themselves before hoping for assistance for others.' I predicted that the future for the event, 'provided that help, harmony forbearance and priority of needs is correctly assessed', must be bright. There was also a report from Fred Duffield, the chairman of the Worstead Church Fabric Trust. A picture, I remember, appeared in the EDP in July 2007 some 30 years later of children riding in a horse-drawn trailer in the village square. The 14th festival coincided with the 600th anniversary of the start of building work on the Church of St Mary; there was also a reminder of the reason behind the festival with an extract from the very first festival programme. As well as listing all the events and timings, the programme also contained a lot about the history of the village and the church.

The 19th festival programme, from 1984, noted the Festival Office was located in the Gypsy caravan but it also recorded what had become another aspect to our festival fund-raising. The opening address said: 'Regular visitors to Worstead Festival are already familiar with the major restoration work which has been carried out on our majestic church. Now this year they will see the start of another venture which is being partly financed by the Festival – our new Village Hall. The foundation stone was laid on June 16th and we expect the building to be completed by the end of the year. But this is not the end of our commitments. There is still work to be done on the church and we also have to meet considerable maintenance costs for it and for the village hall.'

We had repaired the church and contributed to other funds, but now we were helping the village get a long-awaited new village hall. As the festival grew, it was not unusual to attract 30,000 people a year over the three days and then hand out thousands of pounds to deserving causes. The 1985 programme showed how £5,500 went into the Village Hall Amenities Fund. In the notes of the 1989 festival, we commented: 'The Festival is now in its 24th year and so we are eagerly looking forward to our Silver Jubilee next year when we hope to put on something special to celebrate the occasion. Meanwhile, we can look back with some satisfaction on the ways in which the village has benefited from the Festival. Our splendid church has been largely restored; the first stage in the renovation of its organ has been completed; the Queen Elizabeth Hall has been built and paid for; and, because the festival involved the community, it has engendered a healthy community spirit.'

The 1990 event – the silver jubilee for the festival – had an aerial picture of the village on the front cover during the festival showing the church and the new village hall, and the Queen Mother. That programme cost 30p but entry charges were still a bargain. On the Friday they were £1 for adults and children were free; on the Saturday and Sunday they were £2 and 50p respectively. By 2008 that had still only risen to £5 for adults £1 for children. Parking was always free, and still is.

Pipes often formed the soundtrack of the Worstead Festival and the Norwich Pipe Band were regular visitors. It was father who said to me, when I had been thinking about the festival arrangements, that it would sound great having the pipers play at the event as bagpipes would sound well in the narrow streets of Worstead. I said to him 'If you pay for it I am sure we can arrange it!' The band arrived in Holly Grove garden and parked their bus on the green and settled on my lawn. Then they went and played in the streets and father was exactly right on that, they did sound lovely. At the Burns Dinner in 2014 I spoke to the piper and remarked on how lovely it was to hear him play the pipes. I said, 'You probably don't know me but I used to be the chairman of Worstead Festival and we had Norwich Pipe Band play with us several times.' He told me that the Pipe Band always thoroughly enjoyed playing at the festival. I was pleased to hear that from him.

The pipe band was lovely from my point of view and the villagers' too, but perhaps one of the biggest highlights over the years, I would have to say, was in 1995 when the Band of the Coldstream Guards came to the Worstead Festival. It was the 30th Worstead Festival and we were delighted to have reached such a milestone. We did make that clear, particularly to planes taking off from Coltishall or Norwich Airport as they saw it spelled out in big figures in our field near Worstead Station. My farm manager Jon Lowe put the idea up and got people from the village who could do measurements to set out the figures on the grass. They could not have done better if they had drawn it by pencil. He sprayed the marked out area to kill the grass to spell out the message '30th Worstead Festival', which was clearly visible from the air and the success of it was dramatic.

But on the ground, it was the Band of the Coldstream Guards which made the 1995 festival so special. It came about because of the connection between Worstead and the Rous family, which once owned the Worstead Estate before it was acquired by Harold Harmsworth in 1938. William Rous went on to become one of the highest ranking officers in the British Army as Lieutenant General The Honourable Sir William Edward Rous, and a former Quartermaster-General to the Forces. He was commissioned into the Coldstream Guards in 1959 and rose through the ranks and was eventually Colonel of the Coldstream Guards.

The band of the Coldstream Guards march into the square, passing Gavin's old bedroom window in Worstead Manor House.

He arrived in Worstead one day and had a cruise around the estate. When I heard that he had been to visit, I said I would like to meet him if he was up in Norfolk again and entertain him on the estate. I received a nice letter in reply from him and invited him up to attend the Worstead Festival. When he saw it for himself he was flabbergasted, he could not believe what was going on in the village. Before he went home, he said to me, 'If I can help in any way I would like to bring "my little band" up.' I asked him which 'little band' that was and he said, 'It's called the Band of the Coldstream Guards.' I was delighted but then the discussion started about cost. It is a band which at that time would normally have charged £10,000 for an appearance and I had to point out that I couldn't go to the festival committee and say that I was spending £10,000 as that would leave a big hole in the finances and that we were out to make money, not just enjoy ourselves. William Rous said he'd think about it. I eventually got a letter where he said he could bring the band up for £4,000 but I still had to say, 'I am sorry, we could not afford that amount either.' While we would very much have liked to see the band of the Coldstream Guards in Worstead, I wrote to him, I was not sure that the public would appreciate it, or the cost, as to most people it would have just been a band. He must have been very keen to make it happen and see the Coldstream Guards in Worstead because the next I heard from him was that he was able to make it so that we could have the band for £400. I couldn't believe that he was able to drop the price as far as that but I said we would be very pleased to have the band for that price. He was determined to bring the band to Worstead as he was so impressed by what he had seen, and he did bring the band after all. What had happened was that the band was in Norwich for another performance, and so to come to Worstead all they had to do was make the journey from Norwich to us. That was a tremendous gesture and we set it all up. He had a march past and stood on the podium to take the salute and I stood beside him. We fed the band at the school and they said it was the best meal they had enjoyed on any exercise away and all organised by our catering lady, Cynthia Clare. I later learned that Lt-General Rous was ill and he died of cancer in May 1999, which was very sad.

As the years went by, we were inviting new people to help but we were also losing some of the people who had helped us for a long time and we needed more help, reluctantly, from outside the village. A lot of the people who were in it at the beginning were getting older and we were short of catering, although Mrs Cynthia Clare, who was the wife of my herdsman Arthur Clare – who had by then retired – said she would do it and she took it on to make that happen. She was confident that she could handle it and got a good gang of people around her and was extremely efficient at organising the festival catering, which was getting a bigger job each year. Her contribution was one that was recorded in the 1990 programme, which was bigger than previously with its full colour cover. From serving teas from a caravan in the garden at Holly Grove in the early years, demand for refreshments grew as the

festival got bigger. It moved from the old village hall to marquees on the paddock and then into the new village hall, which became the centre of the catering operation. Mrs Clare would take on the planning six months or so before the festival started, ordered 8,000 plates and cups and recruited 50–60 helpers and a band of cooks to

Festival caterers (Cynthia Clare in blue apron).

make the scones and tarts. Her efforts were duly recorded in the 1990 programme, efforts which earned a profit of around £2,000 for the festival. She was one of the secrets of the festival's continuing success at the time.

In 1995, the Festival became a registered charity but while we had still got a lot of enthusiasm there was more and more discussion about costings which were beginning to rise dramatically and that we had to remind ourselves that when we started our view was that we were in it to raise money to restore the church rather than anything else. Some of the attractions we liked to have were costing us a bit of money, even though they went down well with visitors to the festival, so we felt it was good to keep them if we could. But by that time they had finished doing all the repairs that were needed to the church so it could be argued that the original need for the festival had disappeared. It was in 2004 that matters seemed to come to a head with the event, as we approached the 39th Worstead Festival. There were people in the village who did not like the way we did it. They wanted all the money to be spent on Worstead. Questions were raised about what we did with the money and whether we, as the original committee, should carry on or graciously retire and hand over the running of the festival to other people instead. We had supported the Church of St Mary the Virgin over the years, had raised enough money to ensure that it was repaired and that it wouldn't fall down, built the village hall and much more beside and now we were giving to organisations and groups outside the boundary of Worstead. For example, we gave quite a lot of money to Sloley Church and Westwick Church. The way we set up our trust was for the benefit of the Parish of Worstead and in immediate parishes surrounding, which was about four, though we did give some money to North Walsham because there was a place in North Walsham where youngsters could go and enjoy themselves without drinking and we felt it was appropriate to give a donation to them. That was where a lot of village children were going to school so there was a relevant connection.

I had been chairman for 39 years because so much was tied up with the farm originally. While I was happy with that, it did actually cause us problems because we could not start the harvest until the festival was over because we could not go onto the farmyard with tractors carting grain into the barn. I suppose I was saying to myself perhaps it had gone on long enough and that this would be time to stop. It also coincided with my farm manager being asked to chair the new committee, which I think was a tactful move because I got on so well with him.

Between the time we started and 2004, the festival had made a profit of well over £500,000. It had a turnover in excess of £80,000 and made grants averaging £30,000 a year and was attracting 30,000 visitors. But things were changing and we weren't sure whether it was going to continue to make money, in fact the treasurer

Worstead Festival committee in the mid-1970s: LEFT TO RIGHT, BACK ROW:
Lawrence Vine, Tom Howard, Janet Hewitt, Gavin, Betty Fox; FRONT ROW:
Max Carter, Freddie Duffield, Rev. Donald Petit (vicar), Bob Spanton.

had warned us that the following year we might make a loss. We did have quite a good kitty of about £200,000 which had been built up over the years but in the end, we handed over to the new committee on the understanding that they would continue to help the village and we left them some money in the kitty but not before we had given away six lots of £25,000 to the church, school, parish council, weavers, Westwick Church and the village hall. There was a new group of people who were ready to run things if we were ready to get out. That was maybe something they had heard we were thinking about. I thought to myself that they could not run it without my land for parking but I was prepared to listen to common sense and listen to the views of the village, providing they stick to the founding principles of the committee and that they ran the festival as the registered charitable trust that was Worstead Village Festival. So, we ran the 39th festival but never got to the 40th. We dissolved the committee and the new committee took over but I am still involved. I still go to meetings and I am happy to give the fields for use as car parks. I still go to the festival to have a good look around. It has been such a big part of my life and was simply wonderful to have been involved in it for so many years and, with other members of the Worstead community, to help make such a difference.

Chapter Thirteen

OUR GRACIOUS GUEST

*Gavin escorting HM Queen
Elizabeth the Queen Mother.*

My speech before Her Royal Highness the Queen Mother at the opening of the new Worstead Village Hall was, without a doubt, the most important time I have ever got to my feet to speak. It was a very special occasion, not only because we had the Queen Mother in our village to open our new hall, but it showed what we as a village could – and did – do for our community. Having the Queen Mother open the new village hall was significant in itself because she played such an important part in that. I mentioned in my speech that fact, saying to her that she may not quite have realised how significant her role had been through the generous gesture of giving us the Wheatcroft Roses china tea set as a raffle prize all those years earlier.

There had been a great deal of preparation for the opening ceremony, which took place on Monday 29 July 1985, the day after that year's festival ended and although some work still needed doing on the hall, it was already being well used. Building work had proceeded over the previous year or so and I had the honour of laying the foundation stone on 16 June 1984.

There was real excitement in the village for the opening ceremony, and some nerves, as the big red helicopter came into view and descended to land on the playing field. The Queen Mother looked marvellous in a lemon yellow dress and matching hat as she stepped from the aircraft and was met by the Lord Lieutenant Sir Timothy Colman and Lady Mary. As her helicopter touched down, the church bells rang out in celebration. It was a big moment in the village's history and there were a lot of people there to see her. All the main dignitaries from Norfolk were

there too and she was greeted by them, and their wives or husbands, as she arrived at the village hall. In line were the High Sheriff Sir Jeffrey Darell and Lady Darell; Mrs Bensley who was the chairman of North Norfolk District Council and Mr Bensley; local MP Ralph Howell and Mrs Howell; Mr John Mack, chairman of Norfolk County Council and Mrs Mack; the Chief Constable of Norfolk Mr George Charlton and Mrs

Gavin, 4, and Alexander, 2, present flowers to Her Majesty.

The Queen Elizabeth Hall standing at the edge of the new playing field.

Charlton and Mr Max Carter and Mrs Carter. He was chairman of Worstead Parish Council and former secretary of the festival. I, as Hall President and Festival Chairman, was last in line and it was my privilege and honour that day to escort the Queen Mother during her visit. As on every Royal visit she ever conducted, the Queen Mother was marvellous and had time to speak to people in the crowd and accept bouquets of flowers. The crowd clapped and cheered and there were banners saying 'Hello' to the Queen Mother and people took photographs. It had been a wet festival that year, only the second in 20 years of Worsted Festivals, but on the day the village hall opened the weather was fine.

This very special day came at an already exciting and hectic time of my life. I had met Marcia in 1977 and we were married three years later. By the time of the official opening of the village hall, Marcia and I had a family to keep us busy with Gavin (born 15 June 1981) and Alexander (18 December 1982).

As I took the Queen Mother down the line and introduced her to members of the festival committee, the people who had worked so hard to help save the church and then raised enough money to fund a new village hall for Worstead, I was delighted that my family was able to play a part in such a special day. First in line was Marcia, who was then pregnant with our third son, Bruce, and the Queen Mother stopped and spoke to her for a few moments, which was lovely for me to see. Then I introduced her to William Nash, the project leader, and Mrs Nash, our publicity officer; Derek Gibson, the chairman of the hall committee with Mrs Gibson; Peter Duffield, vice chairman of the committee, accompanied by his wife; treasurer David Richardson with Mrs Richardson; and Gordon Yaxley, who was heavily involved with fund-raising, and Mrs Yaxley. Then came another proud moment for me when Gavin, who was four, and Alexander, who was two, presented Her Majesty with a basket of flowers. They were dressed in kilts and white shirts and looked very smart indeed and I think the Queen Mother enjoyed that moment. The meeting and greeting over, it was inside for the formal part of the occasion and it was my role to rise to my feet and welcome the Queen Mother and give my speech.

'Your Majesty, distinguished guests, ladies and gentlemen, a very warm welcome to the parish of Worstead. Welcome also to our new hall,' I said and then reflected on the progress we had made as a community to restore our church and provide a new village hall. I outlined the hugely important role the Queen Mother had played in that, whether she realised it or not. I continued:

> It is a long time ago the seed of the idea was planted. The action really started some seven years ago but the very intense planning and the actual building was over the last two years. As you see it still needs many internal fittings and trim to give it character and take away the bareness. It is rather like a new-born baby without its

clothes. Sorry for the comparison but my life seems to rotate around babies these days. However, the hall is already working quite hard and we are well pleased with the bookings. I have often wondered ma'am if perhaps you had rather more to do with this project than you realise. I well remember when you were so very kind and gave us a Wheatcroft Roses tea service to our festival committee, we had just completed our first festival and perhaps more by luck and brave ignorance it had been quite successful. With that experience we were more cautiously planning another when we received word of your kind gesture. The reaction was immediate. It boosted everyone to a much higher plain of confidence and determination. It taught us to aim high and be ambitious if we were to actually succeed in saving our disintegrating church. Some ten years later, with a major part of the church restoration behind us, it was quite forcibly pointed out that our Sir Harold Harmsworth Memorial Hall, which had served the village so well since 1920, had become very tender indeed. So here we are, another nine years later after a great deal of hard work by a great number of people, still aiming high. Thanks are due to so many people over the years that it is quite impossible to mention names. Our thanks to both county and district councils, to those who have helped with donations, those who have helped with the planning and construction, those who willingly give their time on the fund-raising committees and who have worked so very hard at it. From the willing gestures of help from outside the village to the cups of coffee at the many meetings, often well on into the night, we thank you all very much indeed. Most of the people are represented here today and we hope they will accept this very special occasion as our wholehearted appreciation of their efforts, whether it was a major role or a back-up chore. We have had to encroach a great deal on committee members' leisure time, competing with Crossroads, Dynasty and Dallas. You could say that even old JR could not stop us. We, of course, have had a lot of laughs and made many new friends but the most valuable fact of all is that we have learned to work together and get our priorities right. How lucky Worstead has been to have had so many friends, help from so many quarters. It just could have been, had fate dealt other cards, we would now be patching up an old worn out hall and we might only have a ruin instead of the beautiful building across the road. We could not be celebrating this day at a better time. The church has just had its last big structural repair completed, leaving much to do but smaller items to contend with. This hall, though built and running, still has a clubroom, a verandah and storeroom to be added. At the moment it is being used regularly for badminton, aerobics, dog handling club, Mardlers' Club, Women's Institute and Fellowship with a mixture of dances, 21st parties and wedding receptions and fetes thrown in. We hope it will be enjoyed by all age groups for many years to come. I read in a book the other day ma'am that when you were a small girl at school you had a very simple way of expressing your need for pocket money – you wrote a note home which merely said 's.o.s. l.s.d. r.s.v.p.' It would save a great deal of time if we could adopt your system. We know of your interest in the countryside and agriculture in particular, we read of your travels all over the world and the immense amount of work you get through. What a wonderful example you set. I believe you have a favourite motto which is 'your work is the rent you pay for the room you occupy on earth'. We must all agree that your rent is well paid up. In our 20 years of festivals we have always been exceedingly lucky with the weather but the sun has never shone for us like it has today. Thank you for taking the time to come and see us and indeed for all the public work you take on for us all. You have written yourself into the history book of Worstead. We will never forget you. Your Majesty, I now have great pleasure inviting you to name our hall and unveil the plaque.'

I must have been speaking for seven or eight minutes and at the end of it, the Queen Mother drew aside the curtain to reveal the plaque as she officially opened our new village hall. And then, she honoured us with a speech of her own, which I can record here:

> It nearly is 20 years since I first heard of the plans to raise funds for the restoration of Worstead Church and I am so pleased to be here today to see the outcome of what has been a tremendous effort on the part of this parish. Those early plans developed into the Worstead Festival but as the years passed the momentum increased and money seemed to come in to such an extent that not only has it been possible to save your beautiful and historic church but there have been enough funds to make a contribution for this magnificent new village hall. The original hall was given, as we know, by the late Sir Harold Harmsworth and it was a great boon in its day but I believe as time went on, it was found to be quite far from the centre of the village and maintenance costs became prohibitive. Now, through the generosity of many benefactors, this new hall has been built and equipped. It is a tribute to the enterprise and enthusiasm of everyone in the community and a shining example of what can be achieved when people have the will to help themselves. I do congratulate you most fondly and I now take much pleasure in declaring open the Worstead Village Hall.

Worstead's old village hall.

We were very pleased to hear her words of congratulation and support and have her there as the person to open it. We all knew that without the donation of that tea set for the 1967 festival, none of this may have happened because that spurred us on and gave us the confidence to press ahead which saw the festival grow into what it became. In those early days, there was someone on the committee who was able to arrange for the Queen Mother to offer the half set of Roses china and when we started to discuss who would open the hall, they said that there was only one person who should do it and that was the Queen Mother. I thought that was aiming quite high but she had truly helped us – a lot of people did not realise how much she had helped us at the time – and the enthusiasm came from that. It was amazing. I thought she would not be able to do it but what I did not know then was that she was staying at Sandringham and one of her ladies-in-waiting lived near Neatishead and she used to pass through Worstead on her way to see her, so she knew Worstead.

Our project leader Mr Nash also made a speech, making that point and thanking the Queen Mother. He said:

> Your Majesty, distinguished guests, ladies and gentlemen, it is with pride but humility that I speak today for the people of Worstead. It was some 13 months ago and the hall was still under construction that I wondered whom shall we have to perform the official opening? Many names came to mind but I asked myself who is the most respected and best-loved person in the land and in my mind ma'am there was no doubt.

> At that time it seemed to be a wild and improbable dream but today that dream has come true. As Mr Paterson has said, the hall meant long and hard work for many but your presence here today ma'am has made it all worthwhile. Your love of Norfolk is well-known and I see from the popular press you are now being called the Queen of Hearts. Certainly ma'am you have captured the hearts of the people of Worstead and it is from the bottom of my heart that I thank you for opening our hall, unveiling the plaque and for graciously permitting us to call it the Queen Elizabeth Hall.

At the end of the ceremony the Queen Mother was presented with a gift of a small statuette carved from Worstead wood by a Worstead man before she toured the new hall. The carving was made by a man named Anton Wagner who came from Oberammergau in Germany. He lived locally and I had seen him carving at the festival and saw that there was more than a little skill involved in what he was doing. I stopped and spoke with him and he told me he lived near Aylsham, to which I said it was a pity he didn't live in Worstead, but that was all that was said. About three weeks later, there was a knock on the door and it was him. He said, 'Do you remember me?' to which I replied, 'Yes, of course, you are the wood carver.'

It transpired that he had been turned out of his workshop and wondered if I had a shed he could use, which I had, and he was delighted. I never did charge him for the workshop. Within another three weeks, he came to me again and said he needed a house. I had one empty in Honing Row, so he moved in and was set up with a home and workshop in Worstead after all. He was a big asset to the village and I think over time I've acquired about 20 of his carvings. Anton used wood from the estate and then out of the blue, he said he was going to walk home, all the way to Oberammergau. Before he went away, he brought me one more carving and then he walked off back to Germany. He got there but later I heard he had been knocked down and killed in a road accident in Switzerland.

But it was his carving that was presented to the Queen Mother. In return, she left us a signed portrait of herself as a memento of the ceremony. The hall still needed internal fittings but we had come a long way by that time since I laid the foundation stone and it was so much better than the old hall which was made of wood and had a tin roof. As the Queen Mother was escorted outside again, the crowd began singing 'Happy Birthday' as it was close to her 85th birthday. Of course, there were more bouquets to receive. When the helicopter took off later, it was literally weighed down with flowers!

Father Anthony Long, who had blessed the new hall, walked with the Queen Mother across to the church. She paused to look at the Norfolk sheep that were grazing in the churchyard and were the variety that had provided the wool for the cloth that had made Worstead so famous in the first place. She also spoke to Harry Hambling, the shepherd. Fred and Mrs Duffield were at the church door and inside there were weavers from the St Mary's Worstead Guild of Weavers, Spinners and Dyers, exhibiting their craft. Dan Chapman was also present and village schoolchildren performed with hand bells. As the Queen Mother left, a distant piper played the Queen Mother's March.

Harry Hambling, shepherd.

We had been told by Her Majesty's representatives that they did not think she would be with us more than half an hour but she was with us quite a bit longer than that and I think we entertained her very well. We were all delighted with the way the day had gone; it was marvellous to have the hall opened and running, being used by local people and have the Queen Mother perform the ceremony. It was perfect.

As a festival committee, we had talked on several occasions about a new village hall to replace the old-fashioned hut, which we all knew was neither quite big enough, or indeed, solid enough to last much longer. The parish council was concerned that one day if there was a gale it could get blown away. But it was

Cynthia Clare, who was in charge of our catering, who had made a valid point in the days when we started to think about what else we could do with the festival money and the possibility of considering a new hall. She was saying that people she had talked to had said to her that if you give money to something else – other than the church fund – and something in the village that people would benefit from then you would get more help for the festival. Effectively, she was saying that if you talked about giving some money to a new village hall that might encourage more people to think about coming to help us. And she was right. So we decided to start thinking about a new brick village hall.

I had a builder working for me at the time, and he was doing a good job, so I asked him to draw up plans, which he did. These were plans that the village could discuss and have a look at. By that time we had also formed a village amenities charity and we began putting money from Worstead Festival into the amenities committee. We then had two trusts, one for St Mary's Church and one for the village hall fund, and we were putting money into both of them. The benefit of putting the money in a trust was that nobody could interfere with it and spend it on anything else. We got the plans drawn up and started to discuss them and how big the new hall should be and where we should put it. We travelled around the county and looked at five or six village halls and talked to people who built them to see if they were pleased with them, if they were too big or too small and what facilities they wanted to get in them. So we did quite a lot of homework before we came up with the plans and built it. Advice we got was that if you build a middle-sized one you have increased running costs but often cannot do anything to raise enough money to run it, you have to have one that is useful enough not only to hold events but of a size that you can keep raising money for it. We also found that if you build it too small you cannot get back sufficient money to keep it going. We decided we wanted a village hall big enough to be able to have the catering for the festival once a year and that we would do it in two halves; build one part first and then the second half later to finish it off when we had the funds. As part of the process the village hall land was transferred to the parish council. Before long, and today still, it is used by the parish and various organisations, youth clubs and normal village activities.

I have been on Worstead Parish Council since 1965 to the present day, so will have done 50 years by the end of my current term, which I think will be my last. I joined Worstead when I lived up there because I was involved in other things in Worstead. My view was that if you live in the middle of the village and you farmed in the middle of the village you are under some obligation to be on the parish council. I have been vice chairman of the parish council several times but because of my position I felt that I should not be chairman as it could get difficult if there were issues such as complaints about things on the farm, smells or dirt on the road, though I always tried to make sure there wasn't dirt on the road or footpaths.

I was a district councillor when there was a Smallburgh Rural District Council, which was located at Stalham. I succeeded my father as representative of the parish of Smallburgh on Smallburgh RDC in December 1969 when father retired for health reasons. Ian already sat on the council as the representative for Dilham. That was later amalgamated with North Norfolk District Council. The man who was representing North Norfolk was much more involved and I thought he was doing a good job for the district so I did not think I would stand and oppose him. In Smallburgh, I was able to help with a playing field as well. The playing field they had was not that big. It couldn't hold a football field on it and it had a small village hall and the land was quite a funny shape. It was near my land, so I asked if they wanted to move the playing field, and the wooden hall, to another area of land closer to the houses and they thought that was a wonderful idea. So the village hall was moved on to a better shaped area of land that I gave them and I had the land where the old playing field was, so we did a swap and we both gained from it. They have a bigger area of land now, there is a football pitch on it and the village hall and they are now making a bowling green so it all worked out well for everybody. I was a member of Smallburgh Parish Council for more than 10 years to 1985 and also a governor of Worstead Voluntary Controlled Primary School for several years up to 1983.

I have also been awarded an MBE for public service, though when I received the letter asking if I would accept it, I was not sure whether I would because a lot of people had done work for the village and for the festival but in the end I decided to accept it on behalf of the village. I was presented with it at Buckingham Palace by Prince Charles and took Marcia, my sister Marion and sister-in-law Elsie along to the ceremony and then we had a night at the Farmer's Club in London, with a small dinner party, where Gavin, Alexander and Bruce joined us. I have met Prince Charles several times over the years and was very proud to receive it from him but that MBE was for the Worstead people, and some of them were exceptional.

Chapter Fourteen

THE FARM IS MY LIFE,
MY LIFE IS THE FARM

Back in father's day Wally Botwright was the foreman at Church Farm, Smallburgh. He had taken over from his father Billy and was a good foreman. He used to be a horseman so it was normal for him to be up and about early. He didn't have a car so every morning he would go out first thing on his tractor, head off round the farm and have a look at what things were like. When he got back, he'd go and talk to father outside his bedroom window and say that he was maybe thinking of drilling if it was dry enough or ask whether the land needed cultivating again. Along with Wally, the other foremen on the farms were John Green at Dilham Manor, Donald Bell at Dilham Hall and Billy Smith at Worstead. They were loyal and would have done anything for Dad.

Father would start work at about 6am and talking to his four foremen was how his day began. He would go through the day's work with them, decide who was doing what and have a discussion on the day ahead. While he'd talk with Wally from the bedroom window, he'd generally speak with the others on the telephone. We had a lot of good men working for us under the foremen and it was a two-way relationship and they appreciated that. There were a few language problems though and it was difficult for father because he had this broad Scottish accent and some of the men could not understand him. Sometimes, the men would say to us 'What did your father say?' but they gradually got to know him better and could understand the accent. Father loved working with the men and he loved to see them happy.

It was the same with my foremen. I'd speak to them at the start of the day and set them off with orders for the men. George Goodwin was my foreman at Worstead. He was a very nice man, a cheery man who saw the funny side of life. He would always talk about things going well and he was a big help to me. George succeeded Billy Smith and when we needed a new foreman, it was right to look among the

Gavin's father with his farm employees and their wives.

men for one and he was the right choice and I think when we made him foreman, all the other men agreed.

As foreman, George would go over to the cowshed and talk to the herdsman Arthur and ask if everything was all right. They would quickly go over the day and then he'd go to the stable and give the orders to the men. On many occasions we would go to the cowshed together and talk to Arthur about various bits of his work and go and look at the calves and if you looked on most days you would know if the calves were getting better or worse. We then went out on the farm and saw the men doing the job they had set about and checked that they understood what to do. George's wife used to come and help us in the house as well.

Father never really stood back from farming totally and in many ways he kept his hand in and was running his farms up until the day he died on April 4, 1970. Ian and I always tried to please father because he did so much for us. I would not say it was a big shock when he died, but because he had been ill for that length of time we had been through that part of it already, and there were times we thought that he would have died earlier than he did because of his troubles with illness. However, Ian and I always knew what was going to happen with the farms when that day came. The Dilham farms sat very well together so Ian took those on while I had Manor Farm Worstead and Church Farm, Smallburgh. There was no real talking about it, it was more or less expected that would happen when father died. Indeed that had been the way we had managed when he was ill. The four companies were Smallburgh Farms Ltd, Worstead Farms Ltd, J.A. Paterson and Co. (Dilham) Ltd and John Paterson (Dilham) Ltd. When he died, we just continued to run things the way they had always been run and the way he meant it to be. We each took over two farms, run completely separately with their own staff. The acreage was split about equally too. Looking back on the whole thing, father tried to see that Ian and I were educated but he had tried to educate us in his way of farming and there is no doubt where we got our inclination for cows from. A lot of his principles in that were pretty set and there was no misunderstanding about what he thought.

Asthma left its mark, and then he had his illness and his operation and he had a slightly different attitude after that. He was never a man for going on a holiday and lying on his back in the sun but if there was a show on he liked going back to Scotland, particularly the Ayr Show or the Highland Show, because he'd meet a lot of people he used to know and he loved that.

If the truth be known, he never really meant to come to England but that was what got him started in farming and one thing led to another. That was quite remarkable, to think that he came off such a small farm in Scotland, of about 70 acres up there and most of it hillside and some of it pretty steep – I know, as I'd walk most of it when I was up there on holiday. Within the whole family there was an in-built desire to be successful in life and to work hard. That was traditional in the whole family with my grandmother and grandfather too.

With his change in attitude, father still never went out of his way to say to us 'you have done that well' or praised us, in case we got big-headed. That again is a traditional thing among Scots people, though Snowy Gleave did once give us an idea of what father thought. He said to us once: 'Father says you and Ian have got hold of it and are doing a good job,' but father would not say that to us himself, though I think he was pleased with us.

When it got towards the end of his life, Father could not get upstairs very easily so mother made his bed downstairs. Even then I did not think he was within days of dying but he went all of a sudden. He had achieved very much and what he set out to do and I think that he would agree that Ian and I have lived up to what he wanted us to do. He wanted Ian and me to take over and keep it going and by that time Ian had sons as well. By the time father died it all had been arranged and he would have been happy.

Farming was changing and life on the farm was moving ahead. Gradually, the horses disappeared, though not all at once. Tractors could do the job horses did so much quicker; in time, each job was taken away from the horses and given to the tractors. The last horse job to go was the stock feeding. It could be done by a boy and he would use a quiet horse and cart to go out and cut kale and feed it to the cows. As the older men were retiring we found we were using more and more machinery and we soon saw how much quicker you could do jobs. We had a little light grey Fergie, which was a real boost to our farming. I've still got three of them, one each for my boys. The Fergie – the Massey Ferguson – came with a whole set of implements such as plough, cultivator and drill and a lot of other nippy little instruments and we used it for a lot of the work with potatoes and sugar beet.

With the tractor we had an implement that was a bit like a sledge and we used it to 'squeeze' the beet out of the ground. Before that, we would dig sugar beet by hand with a 'spud' which the men would stick into the ground to lever it out. That would loosen the beet and then you had a man who would pick it up with a hook, cut off the top and throw it into a pile. Even then, it still had to be picked out and put on a horse and cart or tractor and trailer to be taken to a heap on the roadside. There was a lot of physical work in lifting sugar beet in those days but with the tractor, even though the beet still had to be picked up, it was much quicker and you could do two rows of sugar beet at a time. We would also do beet singling to get single plants but you had to be careful not to take too many of them out of the ground. We used the Fergie for the potato crop as well as it was small enough to go between the rows. It would flatten the heaped rows and then bank them up again as that was the best way to get rid of weeds.

The change happened slowly and that was good because you had to get your men trained and capable of driving a tractor and using the machinery before the horses went altogether. We didn't jump into changes but what went first was ploughing as that was hard work for a horse but the Fergie, with a two-furrowed plough, could fly about the field. The horsemen were a different breed to the tractor men but we did get more boys interested in farming when we started to move to tractors. I was sad to see the horses go but we did not have an option; we needed to do jobs so much quicker to keep up, and all four of our farms were going steadily the same way. We had some 60 men working on our farms at one stage. Now we have a staff of six. As Douet comments in his book, mechanisation was having an impact right across farming in Norfolk and investment in machinery rose during the 1950s. At the start of the 1950s a quarter of the county's workforce was directly employed in agriculture, that was some 33,000 regular and 8,500 casual workers but by 1972 that had fallen to 13,000 regulars and 6,500 casuals.

After the Second World War, the number of herds fell in Norfolk. One issue was being able to find enough suitable labour. Good cowmen were hard to find, and still are. The increase in machine milking helped offset some of the labour issues, but the figures from Douet tell the story: in the early 1950s, there were 53,000 cows in about 2,400 herds but that had fallen to 1,000 herds by 1972 with an average of 33 cows per herd.

For us, nothing much seemed to change but slowly we were plodding in a certain direction. Probably the greatest change came through the introduction of bigger machinery that could do tasks much quicker, whether in the cow shed or on the land, but you had to take care as the bigger the machine the more weight it put on the land. A potato or sugar beet harvester today weighs an awful lot, particularly when it is fully loaded, whereas horses didn't put much weight on the land at all.

The main reason for bigger machinery is that you have to farm with the weather, you cannot farm against it. Therefore, when it is good weather you have to go out and cover as much ground as you can and that means that on a sunny day when it is dry underneath you would go out and do the drilling. That would be crucial in getting the crop established. If you mud-puddle it and work in the pouring rain, you do not expect good results. But one thing is certain; whether you have good machinery, good labour, good tractors, and implements it all needs good weather and you have to use the weather you get.

Keeping up with new developments is also very important, whether with new varieties, sussing out prices or new machinery. Sometimes you will get something come in which is a huge step forward. The job of the farmer, apart from working the land and making sure things are done in good shape, is in knowing what to buy and how much you should pay for it. You are spending money practically all the time on fertiliser, sprays and machinery and you cannot keep changing it so you really want to make sure that what you are doing is right and that you can manage the outcome. A farmer needs to know when something is right and when it is wrong.

When Ian and I took the farms on, we had similar ideas in business thinking and we talked to each other about different things such as irrigation, various crops, and what was coming in next. We used to discuss most things that were going on. With Manor Farm at Worstead, when I started to run it, we grew wheat, barley, sugar beet and potatoes and would also grow peas for the Westwick factory and dwarf beans. We grew peas for a long time until the land got 'pea sick' and they did not grow so well so we had to grow beans instead. We're still members of the Aylsham Pea and Bean Group. We worked well together and would always help each other out at harvest time. Ian was a member of Eastern Counties Farming Committee and I was part of the organisation that later became Anglia Farmers. We discussed things, even though there may have been a certain amount of competition with one another. We just continued what had been done before because we had the same men and we knew father had a very good system which stood the test of time and he did not change it very much and we saw no reason to either. The men had been there for a while and they knew exactly what to do.

There have, of course, been changes and challenges over the years; red tape, legislation and new regulations have been a big issue but you just have to keep up with it as best you can. But most of the changes are steps in the machinery world or technical advances. With machinery advancing so quickly we tend to lease equipment such as the combine harvester and we do that for three years because in that time there may be a better one come on the market.

Corn has always been a huge part of what we do and we always knew that one of the big things to get right was the harvest. The combine harvester speeded that up for us – we had the first combine harvester in the district – and we have always tried to keep ahead of the game with farming but particularly with the way we harvested the crop and then stored the corn.

The old-fashioned way with a horse and wagon was to stack it up and we knew once the grain was in a stack the crop was safe. Again, dry weather was critical and if you stacked it in good condition you were sure of your crop. That was the way when I was growing up; it was the ancient way, but it worked. First you had to cut the corn and then stack it together in what was called a stook. It was stacked in such a way that when it rained the rain ran off and the wind would blow through the top and that kept it dry. They were put on a wagon one at a time and carried off the field when you had a good load. That was carted to the stack yard and the men set about building a stack of sheaves and that was all done in dry weather. Once you got it on the stack in good order, it was safe and it would not go wrong then. Rats and mice were always a problem, but vermin was something we had to live with and control. The corn was threshed out of the sheaves on a threshing machine and the corn was then put into bags.

Out at Hall Farm, Worstead, the landlord had built a set of buildings in the village for the harvest. That was when I got started in farming. You emptied the combine into the trailer, took it to the barn and tipped the corn from the tractor into a pit in the ground and an elevator lifted the corn out of the pit, took it upwards and conveyed it into bins and from there you could either dry or dress it. You could condition your corn if it was not quite right.

As well as being my foreman, George Goodwin was my corn man too and he used to spend weeks and weeks working in the corn store. Part of his job was to put the corn up the elevator and in bags and he would then wheel it across the yard to another shed which was just open concrete and put them up two bags high. That shed probably took 2,000 tonnes of corn. But that was a very slow process because you were moving it twice. I got the idea that the big barn in the village – now two houses – would be a good site to put all the machinery that would do the same thing and would store 2,000 tonnes of corn in bins which would mean the sack job then disappeared. That was a step forward; from stacking corn in bags to sell, to bulk storage of grain. The big barn was ideal for that. It was high, it had got plenty of big bins in it and you could go into the roof with the conveyor and had the room you needed to store the corn.

I had that for many years at Worstead and it was a good outfit. I had to manage it and make sure the corn was dry. It needs to be 17% moisture or under. If it is more than 19% the corn could go mouldy. If you understand how corn needs to be treated and preserved and you make sure it is kept right the corn will not spoil. If you get a lot of mould your merchant will not want to see you at all. I used that for many, many years and it worked like a dream but you had to manage it all the time, watching what the grain was doing to ensure it was not overheating or too wet.

The bins would hold about 40 tonnes of corn. Under the ground there would be a conveyor and you could open ducts that ran out of there and onto the conveyor to the elevator. That took the corn up to the roof line to another conveyor and to where you want to put it. You could put the corn into other bins or onto a lorry without a hand touching it at all. That was a big move forward and we had a good plant at Worstead at the time.

The next big corn development for us, and what is used today, was the grain store at Church Farm. From the conveyor system at Worstead, now all we have to do at Church Farm is back the trailer into the shed and tip it up and then we have a pusher on the front of a JCB which will put the grain up into a big heap.

We have an air floor and two blowers to blow air through which takes the moisture out so we do not need to move it again and we can store it there for as long as is required. You can open the ducts and direct the air to where you want, to keep the corn at the right level of moisture. We also have a stirrer with a nine-foot augur that goes into the crop. The moisture rises so if you put that on, it tends to bring the moisture content nearer to the top with air coming up through the corn. The new grain store also holds 2,000 tonnes and is part of a considered programme of modernisation to respond to today's farming needs. We put the grain straight in there at harvest time and aim to sell it when market

Gavin in the new grain store.

155

conditions are right. We try to spread our income over the year. One of the things we always try to do is sell corn in the spring because you often get a better price for it. That also depends on the world market but we do know that people are often getting a bit short of corn in the spring.

Along with adopting a more modern approach to the way we grow and store our crops, we were always updating the way we looked after the cows. With the milking operation there were several steps and we were always looking to improve. The Worstead plant we have now is probably the most efficient I have ever had and we can milk 32 cows at a time. We did have the two herds, at Hall Farm Worstead and Smallburgh, but now we have just one herd at Hall Farm, which is a subsidiary farm. It is away from the village and we keep the cattle there so we don't get complaints over smells or things like that. With the machine milking process we have always been making refinements. All the time you are looking at making the cows more comfortable and happier; you change the food a little bit here and there to make them produce more milk and today there are so many ways of doing that. When you know what works, that is very satisfying.

We have, as all farmers have, had challenges over the years and in 2001 we had one of the biggest with the outbreak of foot and mouth disease across the country. It was very worrying and if you were not careful enough you could lose a herd of cows, potentially overnight. That is a factor that I had to live with and you had to hope to keep that sort of thing out of the door. We were lucky as we were not in a very intensive area where you had herds of cows on both sides of you. Norfolk was lucky from that point of view and there were controls in moving cattle around. The one thing we were not going to do was to go out and buy cattle from the west of England. We had taken all the normal precautions with disinfectant troughs and just took great care. The biggest problem was with sales of what were called store cattle, cattle which are fattened and killed for beef. They have comparatively short lives and therefore owners are not quite so worried about them. It is where you have a concentration of cattle that you are most likely to have problems.

We had built up two very good herds with showing and advertising and our herds were quite well known and they were worth quite a lot per cow. The pitfall was that if you were unlucky enough to get a disease such as TB or foot and mouth, you would have to have your cows killed. I would not have been very pleased if that had happened. BSE is also a nasty thing but not very common and we were tested for it and cleared. We were tested for all the things that you could potentially pick up. TB is not a common disease either but if you get it you cannot sell your milk for human consumption. We do regular testing for all these conditions on the farm and I have tested all my life for TB.

Irrigation has probably been the biggest development on the farm over the last ten years. The farming press has been stressing for some time the need to preserve water and irrigate, which is logical. There are a number of interesting watercourses on the farms. We had a bore just across from Church Farm with water taken a mile or so away at Smallburgh Fen. Another underground waterway runs beneath our land, close to Bunn's Farm. It is supposedly an underground stream running from somewhere in Derbyshire right down to that side of Norfolk. It finishes up going out to sea near Caister. In times gone by, the captains of ships knew where that was and they could throw a bucket over the side into the sea and get fresh water. I have told that story so many times and nobody has said to me that is a load of rubbish.

More recently, we have built our own irrigation lagoon which will hold 33 million gallons of water and we are also passing some of that to our neighbours. Water is stored up during the winter months in the lagoon, which is of clay soil, and that is an important fact as it could cost up to £100,000 more to build if you needed to line it with plastic. We have laid new irrigation pipes from the lagoon and with the new layout of piping and irrigation system we are now in a position to grow vegetables and all sorts of things that we could not grow before such as peas, beans, cabbage and lettuce. The major crops on the farm today are wheat, barley, sugar beet, potatoes, peas and beans. We don't actually grow potatoes on our land ourselves, but let the land for others to grow them. The potato store is at Bunn's Farm in a converted Dutch barn and we let the potato store as well. We have changed the emphasis of farming from producing from the land to letting it to other farmers.

Looking back, I think I adopted my father's approach to farming – and to life – in the main. I do not like spending money that I do not think I am going to have. We have had to move with the times with the farm and diversify. Since we bought the estate we have converted six barns into houses and that is part of the business plan on the property side. We used to be paying out money every year to improve property and now we do not have to pay any money out from that point of view. We have developed what was already there; the cottages are comfortable homes for people living in them, and I have to say that is where we have turned things round. It is diversification. My father liked the idea of cows that provided a milk cheque every month and these properties are like the cows as we also get a cheque every month from them.

One of the big elements of farming in Norfolk, particularly with the Scots, was about helping each other out, either with advice or with practical support. That was the case when father first moved to Norfolk, it has been the case within my life, and it is still the case today. There was a time several years ago that I was in a position where I was asked to help out a close friend of mine and his family, and I had no hesitation in doing so. That friend was Willie Alston, who was not only a very good friend but also a relation of mine. We went to America together as Young Farmers and he flew out to Finland and we drove home in my MG when I went on the Nuffield Scholarship trip. We would often meet each other at Young Farmers and he was a straightforward and genuinely friendly man. Willie had a farm near Norwich but by the time I got involved in his farming activities he was farming near Billockby. We often chatted about farming matters, talking over what he was doing and what we were doing. But Willie had a health problem with his stomach. When we were on holiday or travelling he had to have something to eat fairly regular. He had been worried about his stomach for some time and the doctors had been on at him about it. One day, he said to me that his stomach had been bothering him more than normal and he was very worried. I knew he was particularly concerned because he said to me that if something happened to him, he was wondering what was going to happen to the farm and his family. I knew what he meant straightaway. Willie and his wife Margaret had two sons, Henry and Robert, but they were still at school and still much too young to take on the farm at Billockby and their herd of Holsteins. He asked me if I would be prepared to help with the herd if things got bad or anything happened to him and I said, 'Of course I will, I'd do that for you.'

Sadly, Willie died soon after. I did not get involved with the herd until he died but then I'd go over to Billockby every Thursday and help. I soon came to the conclusion that the herdsman there was not really up to the job and in his heart he knew that. It wasn't long before he left and we got another herdsman in who took to the job very well. My role was to manage the herd, make any improvements and alterations and try to keep the cows in good form. It was a good size herd. I did what Willie had asked of me for as long as was necessary and at some point the idea was discussed that the boys were capable of taking over. When I mentioned to Henry that perhaps he should take over, he duly thanked me for what I had done and took the herd on from that point. What was pleasing was that Henry seemed very happy in his new shoes and he was, and is, very capable. The Billockby herd is still thriving and Henry was confident but I said to him that if he ever wanted to ask anything, I would be there for him.

Today, our farms are still thriving. They have come a long way since the days of the horse and while the big herds of 72 head of cattle are no longer there we still have some cows. I have been involved all my life, since I was a child really, and I am still actively involved in the decisions and management of Manor Farm Worstead and Church Farm here at Smallburgh. The farm is my life, my life is the farm.

Chapter Fifteen

A WIFE AND THREE SONS

As farming methods changed, so did my life. I married, had a family, and eventually moved house. Marriage happened later in life for me. I'd had girlfriends but never got near to getting married. To some extent I was busy and I was always moving on to something else, things came to meet me, I never thought of looking for some of them at all. Marriage was something that I thought would just come along one day. And thankfully, it did.

I met Marcia in 1977. Her parents were from Scotland and were members of the Norfolk Caledonian Society. Her father Tom Cook was a real character who could recite Scottish poems and sing Harry Lauder songs. I can remember the first time I really noticed Marcia was at a Caledonian Society do in the new Presbyterian Church Hall in Norwich. I had in fact known her parents for many years. I liked Tom very much. He was a man who saw the funny side of life; he was in the building business and I think he originally came to Norwich to help with the repairs to the bomb damage and then stayed here in Norfolk as he liked it here. The Caledonian Society was a wonderful organisation for the first generation Scot who missed being in Scotland. It was very successful but when the second generation started to come along it died back a bit as they did not have the same level of interest in it.

I had a dance with Marcia, who is younger than me, and some time after took her out again and it grew from there until we were married in Norwich on 26 April 1980. We were both members of the Presbyterian Church near the Roman Catholic Cathedral and had a reception in the Maid's Head Hotel where we had a lunch and speeches and then we went off to Scotland for our honeymoon. We both had friends there and Marcia still has relatives in Scotland – most of mine had come down here to Norfolk – and we toured the different branches of the family.

In the first few years after the wedding, Marcia and I lived in what was my house at Holly Grove, Worstead, and she became a farmer's wife. She had a house to run, was involved in business decisions and whatever else happened as well as preparing for somebody coming to a meeting or wanting to stop by for a chat on a Sunday. That is what a farmer's wife does. I have heard Marcia say, 'People think I am a lady of leisure, but they should come and see, I cannot help but get involved.'

As the older generation passed on, there was a new generation entering the Paterson family. When our first son, Gavin, was born on 15 June 1981, I was absolutely delighted. In farming you are working for your family all the time; your thoughts are on what can you leave in place for your family and you try and protect that and do a good job. My father, I am sure, was considering all the time how he was going to split everything and for me having a son was exactly what I wanted.

Within a few months of Gavin's birth I lost mother. She died on 24 January 1982 and was buried alongside father in the new churchyard in Worstead. Mother's parents are also buried there as well, in fact the whole of mother's family came down to Norfolk from Scotland in the end; her brother James Alston farmed at Sco Ruston, Rob Alston at Witton and Crostwight and then their parents Gavin (after

The older generation: LEFT TO RIGHT, BACK ROW: *Uncle Rob, Uncle James (Sloley), Aunt May, father James Paterson;* SEATED: *mother, Aunt Belle, grandfather Gavin Alston;* IN FRONT: *grandmother Marion Alston.*

whom I am named) and Marion came down as well. In fact, there is a story that when my mother's parents retired, they didn't want to sell their cows so they all came down by train, the cows as well. Uncle Rob from Witton and Uncle James from Sco Ruston and my father met the cows at North Walsham where they picked them out in turn and had a third of the herd each!

With mother's parents, along with mine, all buried in the new churchyard at Worstead, it is my wish to be buried there too. I walked through it the other day and it was emotional, there are so many people in there that I knew well.

Soon enough, our family grew again. Alexander was born on 18 December 1982 and Bruce followed on 2 October 1985. I had three sons and I was pleased with all my sons, and I decided three was enough. When Bruce was near to being born Marcia said to me 'I am sure it is a girl, it is different.' She now says to people when she hears them thinking like that, 'Don't be too sure.' She also says she wouldn't change any of her boys for girls now.

Mother lived at Holly House on her own after father died and when she went Holly House became empty for a while. We did not come straight up here from Holly Grove, there was a fair bit of tidying up to do. When we did eventually move, Marcia said there were particular things she wanted to have done. Holly Grove was where I had lived and it was a house full of what I had done, so when we moved to Holly House, she wanted this to be her home as well. At that time, where the office is now was still the cottage where the old foreman, Wally, lived. He was with us for a long while and lived in the house for 70 years, so I did not touch the house while he was still here. Wally came when he was 21 and left when he was 91. The cottage is now the office on the ground floor but upstairs it has been converted into a light and airy studio. As a very talented artist, this is where Marcia paints.

Gavin and Marcia on the doorstep of Holly House.

One of Marcia's paintings.

The boys started school and the idea was to try to give them a good education. They all went to school in North Walsham and then went to Beeston Hall and to Gresham's in Holt. We thought they wouldn't board but they got to listening to the other boys and eventually became full-time boarders because they felt they were missing out on the sport and other activities at the weekend, though the boys did get involved in farm life when they were home and they did show an interest in the farm. Our help around the house by that time was Mrs Ann Bunting and the boys got on with her very well. She has been with the family 30 years, helping three days a week with house and office work and other tasks around the home and we made a presentation to her to mark that occasion in October 2014.

Early on with the children we would go to Scotland to visit friends. Marcia has family in the south west of Scotland, I have some in the middle of Scotland and further north and Marcia has some family in Aberdeenshire. When we stayed up for a week or so, we got around most of the people. Some we would see during the day and others we would stay overnight if it was convenient. There was one time when Marcia and I took the boys up to Scotland for a holiday. When we reached the border, we stopped to see the piper. As it turned out, he was having a break, sitting down and drinking a cup of tea. I got speaking with him and told him I had been taught by Campbell Brown from the Edinburgh Police who was an amateur piping champion in Scotland. As we talked, I had an idea. His pipes were resting beside him and I asked him if I could play them. He looked at me, perhaps wondering how good I was, and then he said 'Yes'. I must admit, I never dreamt he would – most pipers never let anyone else near their pipes. So, I picked them up and started to play; I did a slow march and then a quick march and could see him looking at me, thinking that I could play after all. I think I probably convinced him that I knew more about playing the bagpipes than he expected. For me, it was another wonderful experience; playing the bagpipes on the border between England and Scotland.

When the boys got a little bigger we took them skiing. I remember the time Alexander suddenly realised what he had to do to control his speed. We were on the slope and he said, 'Where, are we going now, Dad?' I said, 'Right down to the bottom,' and added, 'Take your time, do not go straight down.' But by that time he had controlled his speed so he turned once and then more or less went straight down but he controlled it and he was so delighted. I was pleased for him too. Bruce has also turned out to be a very good snowboarder. As well as taking the family we went with Margaret Alston and family. A skiing holiday was good fun, we skied every day and the boys used to say that I skied very well, though I never thought myself a good skier.

Gavin went on to Nottingham University to study engineering and during his holidays did work experience with Rolls Royce at Crewe. After university, one of Gavin's friends sent him an email from his father's company looking to fill a graduate position in London. After applying, and passing the interview, he negotiated a year's deferral so that he could travel as he didn't take a gap year before university like many of his friends had done. From that Gavin got a job with Guildhouse UK, a development firm in London. He spent five years working for Guildhouse as a development manager, mostly delivering healthcare facilities for the UK government. During this time, he also achieved a second Masters degree in Real Estate Appraisal, but shortly after the property crash of the summer of 2008, Gavin felt it was time to leave Guildhouse. As well as working with the farm, Gavin is also involved in a charity doing work in Africa. In fact, Gavin and my wife Marcia are involved in the charity – called Yellobric – and founded it with their associate Peter McCallum in 2011 after Gavin and Peter spent nine months travelling by land down the west coast of Africa through some of the poorest and most deprived places on the planet.

During their stay in Abuja in Nigeria, they found themselves confined to a hotel complex car park because of a curfew after the President of Nigeria went missing. The restaurant included live music played by a very talented musician who could play almost any requested song. After eating there every night Gavin became friends with the musician, called Babs. He was self-taught and learnt to play the piano from sheet music that patrons of the hotel gave him. After the curfew was lifted Gavin visited Babs' house on the outskirts of Abuja to see a very different side of the city. He lived in a slum, with no running water, but he did have a keyboard, PC and recording facilities that he used to teach the local kids music. After the tour Gavin donated some money to the slum but realised another travelling companion had hundreds of copies of sheet music on his computer. Gavin downloaded these onto a memory stick and uploaded them onto Babs' PC so that he and his students could learn almost any jazz song they wished. This made Gavin think; he realised it might also be possible to do this with literature with eBooks. That saw them set up Yellobric to try and help educate children and teachers in Africa. Gavin's charity now supports students using digital media so that they can have access to literacy and escape poverty.

By the time Gavin returned from Africa, the farm was under contract, farmed on a three-year deal. He spent six months back on the farm, full-time, helping me to restructure the farm so that we now share the farm with my nephew and his son over more acres to make it economical once more. Once again, the wheel has turned and we had to move with the times. I'm sure my father would have been pleased to see the Patersons farming the land together. Gavin now spends three days on the farm and two days in London, whilst also working for Guildhouse part-time.

Alexander has been on the farm all his working life and has shown cattle and won prizes for them. He is married to Alice and has sons Archie (born 2010) and Alfie (born 2012) and daughter Phoebe (born 2014). Phoebe is the first female born into the immediate Paterson family for 80 years – my sister Marion who

Gavin jnr (TOP) *and some of the pupils his charity helps.*

ABOVE: *Alice and Alexander with their children Archie (born 2010), Phoebe (born 2014) and Alfie (born 2012).* RIGHT: *past, present and future: the author with Alexander and Archie.*

was 80 in 2014 was the last female member of the family before the birth of my third grandchild and first granddaughter.

On leaving school, Bruce attended Harper Adams University, a specialist agricultural college in Shropshire, studying leisure and estate management, but after two years he left and went up to a farm in Scotland. This was run by some of my sister-in-law Elsie's family, Robin and Drew Shedden. Up until the 1980s and early 1990s, they too used to be arable and dairy farmers. Whilst Drew bottled and delivered milk, Robin ran the arable operations but they began to diversify by turning some relatively useless scrubland into a clay-shooting club. Drew later packed in the cows and together they expanded the club into what is now known as Cluny Clays. It has a golf range, clay pigeon shooting, archery, clubhouse and many more activities for the whole family to enjoy. Robin has branched out into a Riding School and Livery Yard in the old dairy unit. Bruce picked up many ideas on outdoor pursuits and the tourism industry while north of the border and he hopes to bring these ideas forward into the Worstead Estate Park one day. He thoroughly enjoyed his time in Scotland and still visits and talks to the Shedden family regularly.

Back in Norwich, he spent a couple of years working in marketing for Bertram's Books before spreading his wings and heading to Australia. Having seen what this great country has to offer, I was quite anxious at times if he'd ever come back. He travelled all over the vast continent and had many jobs and even had a holiday in Indonesia. Whilst working in Darwin, selling 'Thai Fisherman's Pants', he got chatting to a young English couple as he wrapped up the sale. Upon some standard questions of asking where in England they were from and slowly narrowing down

Bruce at home in Norfolk and in Oz with a friend.

their local area, he found they came from Worstead! The husband was in fact the grandson of the babysitter from when he was just a nipper. What a small world we live in. Farming for 88 days was a condition for obtaining a second-year visa back in 2010. Once I knew this was the plan, I knew I had to sit tight and wait for his return. Although it was a melon and pumpkin farm, operating a tractor is much the same wherever you are and that was another of his many, many various jobs Down Under.

Bruce returned on Christmas Eve 2011 and was home for 16 months before he was off on his travels again. In this time he started to learn more about the family business and rolled out a maintenance programme on the property portfolio using many different grant schemes to add value to the current stock. But Bruce had always talked of returning to Canada and the Rocky Mountains since our visit as a family in 1997. With vivid memories of Banff National Park's wildlife, the thrill of a ski season and many great friends from his travels, he settled in the town of Banff for a year. There's no farming up there. However, an accomplished café barista, he soon picked up work in an artisan bakery whilst also exploring the mountains around him through a hazy summer and bitterly cold winter ski season as well as visiting some of the hidden gems that Canada has to offer. I never got to ski the Rockies and I would have loved to have been on the slopes with him albeit on skis, not a snowboard.

Once again I was unsure if he would return, and as he often talks of his adventures I can understand why it was perhaps a hard decision. However, in May 2014, Bruce returned to the farm with a wave of enthusiasm and is always looking for the family business to move forward. If you're not moving forwards you're going backwards. He's now hungry to gain knowledge, training and experience, and not afraid of making mistakes as he progresses.

Over the years, the family had grown, not just my family with our three boys and Alexander's children but other relatives as well. We'd also lost people along the way too as age catches up with us all. But it was a big shock when my brother Ian died in June 1992. He was a clever man, was hugely respected, and he was a sound thinker and spoke a lot of common sense. Marcia was the first aider on the farm and Elsie rang her early on the morning Ian died. Marcia went up there straightaway but there was nothing she could do. He died very quickly. Ian, who was only 65, was a member of North Norfolk District Council at the time and had been so for the previous 20 years. In fact, he had been to a meeting the night before he died. Since his death, the farms have been farmed by his sons James and Alistair who have one each and we continue to work closely with them.

One thing we did begin to realise over the years was that there was a danger of people losing contact with one another, so Marcia came up with an idea that would help them get together at least once a year. That was the Easter Sunday football match. If you look at the families related to us in this area we have a lot of boys; some were older, others younger and some of them go to different schools. If you thought about it, and that is what she did, they did not see much of each other but she thought they should so they all knew each other as they grew up. The boys from our immediate family played football and you do not have to go far in the Paterson and Alston families before you find there is a further shoal of boys. So, the idea of an Easter Sunday get together was hatched and a big part of that became a football match in our garden at Holly House. The invitations would go out and on the day people would start to turn up at our house at about 12 noon. We would have a natter and then we would eat first with a buffet lunch. Most of them could eat well so it was a bit of a feast. We'd let them settle down a bit and if it was nice and bright there would be no rush but we'd get started and get the boys organised into teams and if there were girls they could play too. We usually found we had up to ten a side. I used to take part and would usually act as referee and linesman. It was just a fun game and after a few years we thought it would die a death as they all grew up but they seemed to still want to come so we keep holding it. Once the message gets out that it is on again, they all want to be there. After the game has finished we'd have a cup of tea and the older ones would have a natter and the younger ones would usually go off to the pub and have a drink. There are generally up to 40 of us attending. It has happened every year since the first one and I think the football match part of it started by accident as at the time I was a director of Norwich City Football Club. As the day wore on we'd usually end up with a few of us left, talking about our memories.

Farming is such a big part of our lives and of the landscape of this part of Norfolk and we have always felt the importance of passing that on through the generations. Sometimes, it is a natural process, at other times it may be a little more complicated, but there is always a solution. When my mother's brother, Uncle Rob Alston, gave up Crostwight, he had no children so he left it to the Clan Trust, which he had set up as a means to help young people progress in agriculture through the utilities and facilities available at places such as Easton College. As part of that process, he handed the farm on to Willie Donald, who had come down from the west of Scotland with his family, to manage it. Willie had worked for Uncle Rob and when he retired he said Willie could run it for as long as he wanted. He left his farm and investments to the charity to drive three objectives: to encourage others to follow him and bequeathe farms or farmland that could be made available for those who did not have farms of their own; to encourage young people from all walks of life the opportunity to gain a deeper understanding of agriculture and provide them with support into a career in farming or simply to be able appreciate the farming and food production around them; and to support old people's homes and clubs, looking to provide enjoyment and additional comfort to those who need it.

Ian and I were trustees of the Clan Trust at one stage but when you reached the age of 70 you had to retire as a trustee. We needed to replace trustees and to do that Uncle Rob had tried to get some big Norfolk farmers involved but a lot of them declined. One reason, he suspected, was because he called it the Clan Trust and they all thought that it was only to do with Scots. In the end he had to put relations forward to go on as trustees. Uncle Rob gave everything to that and the Clan Trust is still going and raising money for charity. While we had backed off as trustees when we were 70 we still go to the annual dinner. Uncle Rob was grateful for the support of the trustees and had decreed, 'I would like to think each year that the Clan Trust spends a little money on those who have taken part and I would like to have a dinner party for them.' At the dinner party, we always toast Uncle Rob. We have now got quite a few of the higher up people in Norfolk agriculture as trustees and the likes of those that were put off in the first place are now involved. But there are always members of the Alston and Paterson family on the trust, helping pass on that legacy to future generations of farmers.

The Clan Trust committee: BACK ROW: *Billy Wright, Gavin Paterson, Willie Donald, Gavin Alston (Attleborough).* FRONT ROW: *Ian Paterson, Gavin Alston, Uncle Rob, John Alston, George Wright.*

Chapter Sixteen

ON THE BALL

The Norwich City board: LEFT TO RIGHT: STANDING: *Gavin, Fred Kennedy, Barry Lockwood;* SEATED: *Jimmy Jones, Robert Chase, Alan Scholes.*

It must have been in the early 1950s as I was getting into running my own farm that Norwich City first became a part of my life. It was slowly at first; I wasn't a season ticket holder or a supporter and didn't go to matches on a regular basis. I was focussed on the farm, even on a Saturday, and I was determined to make everything work and ensure that I would not make a loss in the first year. As it turned out I did not make a loss – I have never made a loss. I was concentrating on the business and have to say that I was not particularly a Norwich City fan until father got involved. That came about through his connections, like most of the things that happened to father and, later, to myself.

At that time we were both going to the same places to do business: the Corn Hall and the market, where we would sell cows. It was father's habit to go for lunch at Langford's in London Street with corn merchants and other farmers and a good number of them were keen supporters of the football club. Father turned up one day and said that he had been offered two season tickets for Norwich City and that he was going to take them because a lot of his friends went to the football and maybe he should go along and see what it was all about. He bought the two tickets in the front row – season tickets in A block – and we still have those two seats.

The club, however, wasn't doing so well and it was looking for money. I'm not sure whether or not father put any money into the club, but he did come up with those two tickets and I think he thought it was a good opportunity to do something with people he knew. It turned out he enjoyed football but as he got older he could not walk so far because he had asthma bad and he had to be careful; he didn't want to end up in a muddle when he was out because he had got short of breath so I became his chauffeur. I would drop him off at the ground, and then park the car, and walk back to meet him and we'd go in and watch the game together. That got me visiting the football regularly and I must have got hooked on it. I hadn't particularly been interested in football before, I wasn't a supporter but I had played a bit at school. Once I started going with father I went to most home games, though rarely if ever went to away games in those days as father didn't want to drive far by then. At that time, football was much more straightforward. We were never expecting to hit the high spots. Our ambition was more along the lines of being able to creep up the table a little.

When I first started going to Carrow Road the ground wasn't up to much. There were two sides of the ground with no stands and the toilets were dreadful – people were always complaining. But there were those who wanted to improve things and it transpired that there was this group of people who were putting money up to the club, though with that investment they wanted an opportunity to advise the business and that is exactly what they said to the board. With the club in trouble during the 1950s, this group raised concerns that there were no young people with a seat on the board; the board members were all in their 70s and there was nobody young coming through who was in a position to learn how things worked. A lot of these people thought they knew about football but they did not know as much as they thought they did. What came out of that situation was that they started putting names forward, names of younger people they would like to see on the board. My name had been put forward and I was asked if I would be prepared to stand but in reality it didn't seem like that was going to happen at that stage. Sir Arthur South – who had become a director of the club in 1966 – did ring me up at one point, though my answer to him was not too positive and consequently I never heard from him again. What I did say to Sir Arthur when he said they were looking for younger people on the board was that he should not be 'looking' for them, but that he should already know who they were.

We had become fans by that time and we kept our tickets and were regulars at the matches through the 50s, into the 60s and 70s. I became quite enthusiastic and loved seeing teams like Liverpool and Manchester United play. It must have been in the mid-1980s around the time my son Bruce was born that the first real moves towards me becoming a director of Norwich City Football Club took shape.

I knew who Geoffrey Watling was; he was a nice man and I got on well with him. He was always full of business and what he had not done was not worth doing within the city of Norwich. He was running all sorts of things such as the two big halls in Norwich, St Andrew's and Blackfriars. I was quite young when I first met him. I'd noticed him standing in the corner of a Caledonian Society Haggis Supper. He was listening and watching what was going on; it was that night that Ian and I and the Major piped in the haggis for the first time. But it wasn't until some years afterwards that I had the privilege to be involved with him when he was president of Norwich City Football Club and by that time highly-respected for what he had done for that club. Jimmy Jones was another colleague; he was from Yarmouth from the funfair business, and he was on the board at that time with Robert Chase.

Not long before, in 1984, the club had suffered a setback when the old City Stand, what is now the Geoffrey Watling Stand, completely burned down, so it was still difficult times for Norwich City. But there were good times too. I had been to the League Cup Final in 1985 when we beat Sunderland 1–0 with Ken Brown as manager. It was a great thrill, and though it was a well-taken goal that won the game for us, it was also a lucky one. There was a crowd of us went to the match together and being at Wembley made it a great day as well and the whole thing was a big experience.

Soon after that Robert Chase, who had joined the board two or three years earlier in 1982, came round to see me. I remember that because Marcia apologised as she was not able to entertain him because she had come home from hospital that day having given birth to Bruce. At some stage after that, I got another telephone call. It was Robert Chase again. He said to me, 'We keep getting your name coming up as somebody who might be interested in joining the board.' I told him that I did not know much about football but he did ask me who I thought should be chairman to which I said 'It should be you.' That must have been the right answer and in 1985 he did become the chairman. To be fair to Robert Chase, the amount he did for Norwich City Football Club is invaluable, he was a worker, a real grinder for the club. He had a different way of working with people and we all soon learned that you did not open your mouth too wide but he would go with people, providing they would go with him. If it was the other way round, though, it did not work. But it seemed I was what Robert Chase was looking for. I was from the farming community, I had been chairman of the county Young Farmers and I had showed some of the sort of enthusiasm and ability that he was looking for, so I joined the board in 1985 and I soon found that being on the board when Robert Chase was on it was exciting. The problem with the board was still their age and I suppose they were looking for people – younger people – with energy and enthusiasm.

When I went on the board there was Jimmy Jones, Robert Chase, Barry Lockwood and two others. I do, however, remember very clearly the first thing that happened when I joined the board was the advice from the management on the playing side of the club telling us that the one thing directors do not do is to get involved with the players. Some directors wanted to talk to the players and encourage them but he was dead right, directors could not get involved in that side of it. During my early time on the board it was a challenging period. It was at the time that we had to bring in all-seater stadiums after the Hillsborough tragedy. That was one of the first things we had to do. The problem at the time was money as we were just a run-of-the-mill club in the old Division Two. The club did at least own the ground, it was not owned by Norwich City Council, though that was suggested at some stage.

The pitch wasn't in good condition either. The goal areas were one big area of mud and there were other bare patches, it was very difficult to play decent football on it. Now, we have got such a good pitch but when I got involved they did not even water the pitches properly. The first thing I suggested to Robert Chase was that we put some sort of sprinkler on it. In the meantime and unbeknown to me, he had investigated the idea and the next thing I knew they were putting a sprinkler system in. He wanted things to be right at the club and I have to say that he was a man who made sure things were right, nobody worked harder at the club than him, I could not fault him for that and I still think he has not received enough thanks for what he did. The club is now in a super state compared to what it was then. Not long after I started, Robert Chase gave us all an angle to be involved in the running of the club and my job, as a farmer, was to grow grass on the pitch, which back then – as I have mentioned – was not that good. The first day I went out on the pitch, this voice bellowed out from the back 'Get off my pitch!' I was being told in no uncertain terms by the groundsman to get off his treasured pitch. But it wasn't long before someone told him who I was and he soon came up to me and said 'I'm sorry, I didn't know it was you.' We always got on well after that. The pitch was not good but we worked to improve it with our sprinklers and heating so it would not freeze and result in matches being called off. Our pitch was soon in good shape. About that time the Arsenal pitch was always regarded as the best in the league and one year, when they were judging the state of the pitches, we came second to Arsenal which was quite a compliment. When we went to away games, I would always try to sneak out of the door and go and find the groundsman and have a chat. I would talk about the pitch, have a look at it and find out what they were doing, what they were thinking about doing to it and how they were working to improve it. I went to nearly every ground looking at the pitches, to learn more about them and make sure Norwich had a really good pitch to play on.

Just after we started that, the chairman thought we should invite members of the city council along to a game as our guests and we would be available to talk to them. That was when we were building a new stand and they were also interested in how the pitch was dealt with. One young couple approached me and asked how I became involved with Norwich City Football Club. I said, 'I am a farmer and they wanted someone from the farming community to be represented and they wanted somebody who knew how to grow grass, someone who breeds calves and was willing to put calves on the pitch in the summer time.' Well the girl laughed out loud but her partner didn't get it at all, he just moved on to the next question.

While being a director of Norwich City was a serious business we did have several lighter moments. One day, we caused a little stir with father's Rolls Royce. Mostly, the directors would turn up in ordinary cars, people would not throw their weight about much, but Robert Chase did like to bring his Rolls Royce in. Jimmy Jones had one too and would park his Rolls in the club car park. I had made inquiries as to who they belonged to, and thought I'd create a bit of interest.

We'd still got one sitting in the garage at home – in fact it's still with us – it was father's last car. It was a twin blue Silver Shadow, a pale blue and deeper blue. For a bit of fun, I took it down one day and parked it beneath the window by the club. Well, it wasn't so long before people were asking who the third Rolls Royce belonged too as they could all see it from upstairs. It caused a bit of a laugh. To this day, I still drive it now and again. It's a big old thing and sways about a bit.

At Norwich City there was always a difficulty hanging on to our managers. If you got a decent manager they were usually in demand and it was so much harder to hold on to a good manager but now we have a better club with better facilities, perhaps one of the best pitches in the league and well-equipped for the TV cameras, we can hold onto our managers a little better. Robert Chase did see the attraction of having such good facilities. We got to know the managers well over the years – Ken Brown, Mike Walker, Dave Stringer, John Bond – but you weren't close friends with them at that time.

As directors, we mostly went to every game and some youth games as well and that was pretty time-consuming. It was important to go to youth games, partly because it shows that we were interested in what the youth team was doing but also because a lot of the directors thought that the youth side was our main supply of new players and they would come through the youth team if we encouraged them at that stage. Midweek games were particularly time-consuming as we would travel to them and not get back until late. That was not good for me because I liked to be about in the morning fo rthe farming. We went to all the major grounds as we went up and down the leagues. I haven't been to every ground but I've been to most of them. We liked going to the London clubs and they liked coming to us. There was one director who took a liking to the pies, which were specially made for the directors at Carrow Road, and if there were any left over he always asked if he could take them home with him. You met a lot of different personalities being a director and going to the different football clubs but there was one club in particular – I'm not saying which – that always treated us as the enemy. As far as Norwich was concerned, we were not like that and when they came to our club they were entertained as our guests and treated as guests. Robert Chase saw all the teams coming to Norwich as our guests and he went to no end of trouble to make sure they were looked after. As far as the business side went, the best thing he did for the club, in my opinion, was regarding the property. He had the foresight to buy property and the land around the ground, areas where they are now building flats. There is still a lot of property around connected with the football club and that has really helped with the finances.

On one occasion when we went to Manchester United, I recall as directors we walked past the bar and were invited to have a drink. I was the last in line and once I had my drink the barman said to me that he had not seen that before, a club where all the directors only took soft drinks. I said 'We don't celebrate until after the match.' We did win that match and I said it to him again on the way out, though I don't think he appreciated the joke. When I was up there I used to go to talk to Sir Matt Busby. He came from across the moor in Scotland where father came from and I would talk to him about it and we'd have a good chat. He was one of the great men in football who had foresight; he knew long-term what he was going to do.

I enjoyed being a director; I cannot say I was a fanatic and in some ways it was perhaps better not to be a fanatic. I did not interfere with the staff: they were paid for a job and expected to do the job. That was what the assistant manager believed and he was right. I did get to know some of the players later on; I still talk to Martin Peters when he comes to Norwich once a year. I look him out and shake his hand; he was such a good player, a wonderful controller of the ball and he could control a game. There have been some great moments I remember during my time with the club such as Robert Fleck scoring at Chelsea. He was way out from the goal and he clouted it and it went straight into the net. Of course, I also saw Justin Fashanu's goal against Liverpool. That is what sold him, the reason Nottingham Forest paid £1m for him. Looking further back, Bill Punton was an exciting player to watch and I always enjoyed seeing him play for Norwich and I got to know him quite well over the years.

Of course, the great adventure was when we got into Europe after we finished third in the Premier League. It was Dave Stringer's side, though he was not the manager by the time the campaign in Europe started. He was a centre half and came up through the side to being captain and then the manager and he put together a very good team. I still think that was one of the best teams Norwich has ever had and the atmosphere when they played was magic.

Our first game in the UEFA Cup was against Vitesse Arnhem. When we went over there we visited the war cemeteries. It was quite an emotional trip because of the build-up and the fact that it was our first venture into Europe. It was exciting too – the club was excited about being in Europe – and I enjoyed the whole trip, and we won. After the match in Holland some of the company went home but we went straight off to Switzerland for the draw for the next round. But there was drama with the plane carrying the wives back to Norwich. It overshot the runway, though only by a few yards. We knew that something had gone on and we were trying to get messages through and make telephone calls to check that everyone was all right. Marcia was fine and she said it was a lot of fuss about nothing.

When we learned we had got Bayern Munich in the next round the atmosphere was that our European adventure had probably finished, but we beat them and our team was worthy of the win. We won 2–1 in the Olympic Stadium in Munich when Jeremy Goss scored that special goal and then held them 1–1 in the return leg at Carrow Road to win the tie. The whole team, managed by Mike Walker, moved back and forth over the pitch together and that was the key to the win. I think we hoped we would get through the match against Vitesse Arnhem but perhaps we expected to get beaten by Bayern Munich. It was such a great experience and we knew that we were enjoying Europe in the way that all the big teams were doing with dinners at both ends and so much more going on around the ties as well as the matches themselves. Then we played Inter Milan. I remember so clearly being in the San Siro stadium in Italy. We were sitting behind the Italian directors and we were playing very well. The whole team seemed again to be moving as one, which was the key to success in all three matches. They pulled a bit extra out of the bag and they were beginning to look like they could win it. The Italian directors were fidgeting about and I will never forget how worried they were that they would get beaten. Inter Milan, who eventually won the cup that year, came to us first but in the end they beat us 1–0 in each game and we went out of Europe.

One of the most interesting footballing opportunities we had through Norwich City was the chance to go to the 1994 World Cup Final in America. England hadn't qualified that year, which was disappointing, but a crowd of us from the football club still went over to America for the latter part of the tournament. As well as the football, we did some sightseeing and met people and went to some events, most notably a concert by the Three Tenors – the Spanish singers Plácido Domingo and José Carreras and the Italian singer Luciano Pavarotti. It was held at the Los Angeles Dodgers Stadium the night before the World Cup Final. We sat at one end and were amazed at how the stadium had been decorated for the concert with plants and waterfalls; it was magnificent. When offered the tickets for the Three Tenors, we realised it was too good an opportunity to miss. Geoffrey Watling came with us to that show, he was very keen to see it, as well as other members of our party. We hired a big taxi and with the driver there was myself, Marcia and Geoffrey and some other people from the club in it, including one who was particularly well-spoken. The driver was Texan through and through and spoke in this big American drawl. Well, it was so funny to hear this conversation. We sat in the back and roared with laughter; a well-spoken English voice asking a question and the response coming

The 1996 Norwich City board: LEFT TO RIGHT: STANDING: *Barry Skipper, Michael Wynn-Jones, Michael Foulger, Gavin;* SEATED: *Roger Mumby, Barry Lockwood, Geoffrey Watling, Delia Smith, Martin Armstrong.*

back in pure American. We couldn't keep a straight face. The concert was fantastic, Marcia enjoyed it very much but for me it was the decoration at the stadium that was so special about the concert, the lights and a waterfall either side and greenery everywhere. The next day, we went to watch the World Cup Final, between Brazil and Italy, which was played at the Rose Bowl, at Pasadena near Los Angeles in California. It wasn't the best game of football you'd see, and it ended 0–0 with Brazil winning on penalties.

Eventually, I did come to the conclusion that I was spending a lot of time on the football club. It was at the time that Delia Smith and Michael Wynne-Jones came onto the board having bought all the shares from Geoffrey Watling. I was surprised he sold all of his shares. I thought he might have kept ten or a dozen or so back. It was in my mind that one of these days Delia and Michael will say they would like to bring somebody of their choice onto the board but I knew we were all full up with our maximum number of eight directors. I made it clear to the Chairman Barry Lockwood that when she did say that, he was to ask her to talk to me because I was prepared to retire and that is what happened. She came to me and said that she had spoken to Barry about it and understood that I would perhaps be willing to give up and I said I would. I had been on the board for 12 years and it was time-consuming at certain times of the year.

She said they would offer me a small dinner party and that I could come to matches, if I wished, at any time. I was given a plaque to say that I had retired and that I should get two tickets for the rest of my life. I was fairly pleased with that. I left the board on 12 May 1998 as a life Vice President. At the time I was sad to leave the board but I could see that things were going to have to change and I thought that I might be better out of it; I also had things to do on the farm and I could only do so much with my time. I still go to every home game and sit in the directors' box. What I did enjoy was going to other clubs and meeting other people. There are a lot of wonderful people in football who work hard for the game, though there are a lot of rogues as well! When you are a director you have a lot of responsibility and sometimes you cannot really be a fan because you have those responsibilities and that may be the difference. But now, I can be a fan of Norwich City after all.

Chapter Seventeen

SELLING THE HERD

Cows have been my life. I have bred them, fed them, showed them and sold them and they have given me a great deal of pleasure over the years. I have been successful and was also very fortunate to have my father pass on his knowledge and expertise to myself and my brother Ian. But as I got older, times changed in farming, more regulations came into play and there were ever greater challenges and demands, meaning I had to begin to think about the serious decisions concerning the future of the Lyngate herd that had been such a huge part of my everyday life.

First, however, I would like to reflect on one of the most remarkable experiences of my life involving cattle. That was the Calgary Stampede, among the most exciting and exhilarating events I have ever seen, and I am so pleased that my family were able to share that with me. Going to the Calgary Stampede is something I had wanted to do all my life though I never actually thought it would happen. But it turned out that there was a farmer who was having a sale at the time of the Calgary Stampede and I decided I would get a catalogue for it. What was better still was his offer to acquire some stampede tickets for us. He set the whole thing up so we went out to Canada, as a family, in 1997 and made sure we got there well before the stampede started because we wanted to spend a little longer out there and do more than just watching the events. We found ourselves booked into a ranch. I am sure it was not really like one of those big ranches you see on the films but it was a ranch with horses and they ran it like a hotel. When we got there and were settled in, they told us we were going for a ride. I looked around the family and said to the boys, 'Do you think you can hang on?' The boys were all old enough to ride; they might have fallen off, but the people there were looking after us very well and nobody fell off and we went off for a ride and I was really chuffed with that bit. They were riding ponies but the ponies knew the drill better than we did and everything was fine.

The next morning we stood in the house with the rancher, who clearly had his own method of cooking, and his idea of portions. He said to us, 'What would you normally have for breakfast?'

'Bacon and eggs,' we replied.

Well you've never seen such a frying pan, it was about half the size of the table and he stacked bacon and eggs in it and it was all cooked just like that on the pan for our big breakfast. Having been well fed and with our tickets ready, we then went off to see the stampede. There was a display of men riding bucking horses, just like you see on the television. The rider gets on in a crate and when they open the door and let the horse out he is supposed to stay on for so many minutes. Another part of the show was the chuck wagon race. These chuck wagons each had four or six horses and were all racing each other. How they did not end up killing people I don't know, it looked terribly dangerous to me, and they were going so fast and the cowboys racing them were all just like you would see on the films.

Then the sale I was interested in came round, and I took the opportunity to go across to the auctioneer to get a catalogue for the boys to look at as they were also interested in what was going on. We sat across from the auctioneer and there was another caller on his left hand side, one in front and another on the right hand side and they were trying to get people to bid. If you made a bid, they would try to get you to make further bids. That was the way it worked. I'd had a good look round the cattle before the sale started and I had this tip off, but I had thought that I would buy something just for fun anyway, though I didn't say anything of my plans to the boys and Marcia. The auctioneer took a look around and he was 'shouting, shouting, shouting,' and then the auctioneer said 'Do I have a marker?' (an opening bid) and so I made a bid of my own but without being seen by the family. As this went on Marcia turned to me at one stage and said, 'There's somebody near us bidding.'

Without letting on, I said, 'There may be. Not everyone who makes a bid flaps their arms around, do they?'

She was convinced someone was bidding but couldn't see who and a few moments later said to me again, 'I am sure someone over here is bidding.'

In the end I did get the heifer I was after. I bought the animal and said to the people at Calgary that I wanted them to look after the animal for me. They did take good care of it and in due course it came over to England. It was an empty Holstein heifer I had bought and that family is still with us. When I eventually said to Marcia that I had bought it she thought I was joking because she said later that I hadn't shown much of a clue that it was me doing the bidding. I am glad I did it – it completed the picture for me. I think the sale was good for the boys to see as they were interested and it made it all worthwhile, not only going to a sale in Calgary but actually buying a heifer. And then it was back to the action of the stampede in the big arena. That was very dangerous looking stuff. Part of it was about riding horses while another part was with cowboys who had to lasso calves and pull them down and tie their legs. It was all very exciting for me as I have been interested in the Calgary Stampede from the time I had been keen on my own pony; it was something that I knew if I got the chance I would go to it. It was exciting but very dangerous too. Probably the chuck wagon race was the most dangerous part; they went hell for leather, beside each other, behind each other and if a horse went down the whole thing would go down with it. I think the boys were thrilled to see it, they have never seen anything like it before and nor had I.

Because of the breed of cows that have been integral to our pedigree herds, one of the constant factors throughout my farming life has been my connection with the Holstein Society. I first became involved with it when I was quite young, probably a member since I was 20. There was a lot happening with us and the cows at that time. Father had built up four strong herds and they were good cows – he wouldn't stand for anything less. He had a saying, 'No feet and legs, no udder and teat set – no cow', which is a phrase I have tried to follow. It was about the time we went pedigree and father bought some Ayrshires for Ian and we also had some pedigree Friesians and put some of them in the Lyngate herd which I had taken over. A lot of those families are still there and I have bred from those families and tried to improve them. Over the years, father said that he always had great pleasure from breeding a good cow and that was carried on by my brother with the Ayrshires and I have done that with the black and whites. They were British Friesians when we started and we converted to Holstein which is a slightly different breed with more milk production and not so much meat. That was the beginning of our pedigree herds and both Ian and I must have done well because I suppose the major thing that happened to both of us was that my brother became President of the Ayrshire Cattle Society and I became President of the Holstein Society in 2004. Ian actually became President of the Ayrshire Cattle Society in May 1976 when he had around 230 milking cows on his farms and his appointment followed his success at the 1975 Royal Show at Stoneleigh where he took the Ayrshire female and breed championships. That was with a nine-year-old called Dilham Manor Tilly Dilly 3rd. I think Ian and I being Presidents of our respective societies capped father's involvement with cows.

It was originally the British Friesian Cattle Society and that is what I joined when I started farming on my own and when we started to grade up the cows. We had already got good cows and they were inspected by the British Friesian Cattle Society as Grade As and from there their daughters and granddaughters were eventually full pedigree. It was progress and I think it made our farm as good as any other. We were already interested in cows and wanted to breed good cows to produce milk but upgrading them pushed that through to another level of value and also aroused our interest in showing pedigree animals. It was time-consuming because there was more paperwork but for that you got a more valuable animal and if you got very good at it, it would be a much more valuable animal.

We have a Norfolk Breeders Club of the Holstein Society and most counties or areas of England also have

ABOVE: *Gavin at the Norfolk Holstein Club stand.*
BELOW: *A line-up at the British Friesian Cattle Society.*

their own club and there are quite a lot all over the UK. I remember in the year after father died, a new cup for Norfolk dairy farmers was presented in his memory at the annual dinner dance of the East Anglian British Friesian Breeders' Club Norfolk Branch. The cup, donated in memory of the late Mr James Paterson of Smallburgh – my father – was for a new female family competition for cows and two daughters. There were some 450 people there for the occasion at the Norwood Rooms in Norwich in February 1971. As it turned out, I won the cup with one of my cows, Lyngate Trixie 7th! On that night we also won trophies for the main herd class and bull progeny competition.

What was also special was that the trophies we had won at the last Dairy Show the previous October were also on display.

With the Holstein Society, there is a national body, based in Rickmansworth in Hertfordshire, that registers all the cattle to keep it under close control. We have always kept very detailed records of our cows. We used to sketch cattle at one time. When I registered them I drew the outline of their markings on the calf's tear-off ticket. Eventually, the authorities stopped the need for that because it was too much trouble but we still do it, though now we photograph them. That was the way of identifying the animal and then we'd put the ear markers on and the sire and family and mother's line. I can take a bundle of these drawings and would recognise the animal in the field from them. We would record the dams and grand dams and I used to put notes on certain ones if they were very good, excellent or show animals. It was just a remark or a couple of words that gradually built up my knowledge of each animal. It is something that I needed to do, to have the level of knowledge I wanted of each animal. If I was not going to keep them, I would use that system to pick the ones I wanted to keep. There were certain families that I wanted to perpetuate; it is about the deeper management of the dairy herd and this would be the future of the herd at that time. There are probably 100 young stock on the farm at the moment, all bred by certain bulls and you start to look at what they are looking like before they have their first calf. Once they have had their first calf you have a better idea of the cow.

Within our branch of the Holstein Society, our club arranges meetings throughout the year and holds stock judging sessions so that everybody in the club has an idea of what a good cow should look like. A lot of it is the same as with any other club, which is friendship, and to me that was a major factor. It was about relationships where you can have discussions with all these other people in the same boat as I was and people that had the same interest as I did.

At one stage I did start playing golf as an interest but it didn't last so long. We used to go and play at Cromer on a Thursday afternoon and seven of us would play together. In the afternoon we were not in anybody's way, we played golf and had a natter and a laugh and would finish before the evening players wanted to get on. A lot of those seven are now playing all over the place and are very good but I realised I wasn't that interested and if I had any spare time I'd rather go and look at a bunch of heifers. I might have kept at golf, but that damned little ball would not always do what I wanted it to do so I never became a golfer. They say golf can improve your business, but for me keeping records and being involved in the Friesian and Holstein clubs – and similarly my brother with the Ayrshires – was what we knew could improve our business. As National President of the Holstein Society in 2004, I would go to meetings nationally, attend meetings at central office and visit clubs all over the country and it was a great honour for me.

However, I knew I was getting on a bit myself, and it was about that time that I realised I needed to go to talk to an expert about my heart. That would have been in

2007. He said that I had a heart valve that 'slurps' instead of beats and to put it right I would need another valve. Just chatting about it like that took the sting out of it for me and I did not feel quite so worried as I had been. He said that I could either have a metal valve or a valve from pig; or as he joked, in my case probably I'd prefer a valve from a cow. I had an animal valve in the end. I was upset at the thought of the operation but as the thing progressed they made me much more aware and comfortable with it and I was fine. When they brought me back from the operating theatre I was a bit doped up and I soon got pretty fed up with seeing the nurse come round the corner with a big needle but she said to me that overall I would look back on the experience as it being exactly the right thing to do. I did not really feel a lot of pain either, considering I'd had open heart surgery at Papworth Hospital in Cambridge. They told me that it would do me until I was 90 and if I needed another one they would do that as well.

While I had the honour of being President of the national Holstein Society in 2004, I remained as President of the Norfolk Holstein Society right up until the autumn of 2014, when I decided it was the right time for me to step down. Originally the President of the Norfolk Society – which was formed as far back as 1949 – was a member who was one of the leading lights of the British Friesian Cattle Society in those early days, Captain Richard Buxton. When he died, he was followed by Mr J. D. Alston. I followed Alston as Norfolk President and before I was President I was also Chairman of the club. Considering Norfolk is an arable county, the Holstein Society is very active. It is a well-run club and its strength is its people.

We worked very closely as a farm with J. D. Alston, who was Uncle James's son, and we had 12 sales together. In fact, we had an annual sale and the deal was that we'd hold it at each other's farms on alternative years. So every second year the sale of Friesians and Holsteins was held at Bunn's Farm and after the sale we would have a lot of helpers and they came back for drinks in the cellar at Holly Grove, which I had converted into a sort of nightclub. Uncle Rob was always where there was a party and he'd sing. He did not have a sale but he was fascinated with ours and he'd come along and then contribute and sing a song or two.

We had two herds and we had a lot of surplus animals and we didn't need to keep them all so we had quite a few for sale. We used to sell 130–150 between us and that made it worthwhile. The sales would be in the autumn and people would come from a long way away to attend and they were really quite successful.

With those factors, my age and my health and taking all things into consideration, I had also begun to think about the future of my milking herd and by 2011, I had made the decision that it was time to sell my beloved cows. The 2011 sale was triggered by a number of things but it was probably the changes to slurry regulations that started it off. There were also other risks such as foot and mouth disease and TB. We have been TB-free for years but if you were unlucky enough to get somebody bring TB to Norfolk and your cows caught it, they would be killed and you could lose an awful lot of capital asset; it worries me is that there are still people who are not careful enough about what they do.

So in my 60th year of farming in Norfolk I sold my 241 head of cattle. The sale was scheduled for Tuesday, 25 October 25 at Beeston Castle Auction near Tarporley in Cheshire and it was overseen by Wright Manley. We had a catalogue put together for what was billed as a 'Dispersal sale of the entire milking portion and close calving heifers from the Lyngate Herd of Pedigree Holstein Cattle, 241 head, the property of Worstead Farms Ltd (Gavin Paterson MBE)'. They were all for sale by auction under Holstein UK Auction Rules. I wrote an introduction to the Lyngate Herd, which was a short history of our background and the herd. It went along these lines:

> As far back as I can remember the family was always immersed in cows, not surprising because father and mother both came from small dairy farms in West Scotland.
>
> In the early days at Worstead, we milked 72 cows by hand, that took a lot of milkers but labour was available who needed work. Gradually, as time passed I got more involved, many of father's friends were dairying as well and chat between them was an education itself. 'It does not cost any more to feed and milk a good cow as it does an ordinary cow'.
>
> At that time all our milk went to the Co-Op in Norwich, they wanted TB free milk for the third of pint for Norwich Schools to drink. The cows expanded and soon with the help of milking machines we had four herds of 72 Ayrshires and Friesians. TB free Ayrshires were often brought in as they could be found in truckloads from West of Scotland as father still had contacts back home.
>
> My brother Ian (John) arrived home from College and asked to have all Ayrshires. So father bought some pedigree Ayrshires to help start off his herd at Dilham Hall. With that in mind, he soon did the same for the Friesians – in 1942 the Smallburgh herd was registered. When I came home from college in 1950 the Lyngate herd was registered in 1952.
>
> My father had a saying, no feet and legs, no udder and teat set – no cow, which I have tried to follow. The theory being that cows do not last long if the back end is not long wearing. After that it is how you manage and feed the cows to get profit.
>
> Our Young Farmers' Club was very active in 1952 – a busload of us went to the London Dairy Show to see cows and new equipment. On my return I gave my father, who had been ill, a detailed report of who was showing and winning, at the end of

this report I said 'I think we have cows in the cowshed out there just as good' to which he replied 'If you really think that you better get started and have a trial run.' We did and in 1953 with the help of George Clare, herdsman, we took Smallburgh Brenda and Lavenham Cherry to the Show. Winning the Supreme Champion with Smallburgh Brenda at the Royal International Dairy Show was the start of our pedigree interest.

We continued to show at the London Dairy Show with varying success until the last one in 1970 with Lyngate Carlink II, she had been three consecutive years before to London, the fourth year she was lucky enough to win the Supreme Individual Champion. Great credit to Arthur Clare who managed the cows so well on those occasions. I was very sorry the Dairy Show stopped as I felt all competitors learnt a great deal to spend concentrated time with their cow and other keen herdsmen, passing ideas and knowledge to each other – what an education.

Holstein Blood has now been used for more than forty years and we have a great choice of bulls to use now with AI – picking the one to use is not easy. We have been lucky with quite a few and have used some homebred bulls from our better cows, which have done well. They used to say 'the bull is half of the herd, his daughters will be the future of the herd.'

So where does Lyngate go from here? The prefix is still alive and the Youngstock have still to unfold.

Marcia and I have enjoyed the tremendous friendship and interest which has come from breeding and keeping pedigree cows. The enthusiasm of our Norfolk Breeders Club has been remarkable for an arable County and is still going strong. The help from Rickmansworth in the past and especially recently has always been very helpful. All farm staff, especially herdsman Shaun Clarke, Hayley Rushworth, Ivan Spooner and Alex, my son, have been working very hard to set the Sale up.

I do hope the cattle do well in their new homes.

GAVIN PATERSON

My words were followed by the Auctioneer's Foreword and he said some very kind things:

Gavin Paterson, MBE, a great stalwart, supporter, and indeed, gifted breeder of Holstein cattle has decided to cease milking on his farms based at Smallburgh and Worstead in North East Norfolk. The decision to sell has not been easy; his beloved LYNGATE herd of Holstein cattle has played such an integral role in his life, the decision to stop milking has been tough but has been mainly driven by the major investment needed to comply with the new NVZ regulations coming into force early next year, and Gavin, at his time of life, feels that it is not right to make that commitment now.

The catalogue looked at my history and success with the cows, my MBE in 2006, being elected President of Holstein UK in 2004 and being a director of Norwich City Football Club. By the time of the sale the cows were being milked in one herd at the dairy unit at Worstead all under the Lyngate prefix, though the auctioneer noted how for many years two herds were kept until the Smallburgh herd merged with Lyngate in 2006. For the last 14 years of my ownership of them, they were under the day-to-day care of head herdsman Shaun Clarke who had taken over when Arthur Clare retired.

The auctioneer continued:

> There is no doubt that this is certainly one of the best herds of Holsteins to be sold anywhere in the UK this year; the cows are in tremendous form and I have to say it is, without doubt, one of the best herds I have ever had the pleasure of selling.

The catalogue listed the classification scores – 41 Excellent (including 20 from 92 to 94 points), 79 Very Good, 54 Good Plus; it then highlighted some of the outstanding individual cows being sold: Lyngate Shottle Jane, Lyngate Destiny Rose, Lyngate Jordan Honey, Lyngate Ross Jenny and Lyngate Jacko Handsome, along with a full resume of prizes won at the Royal Norfolk Show and in the Norfolk Herd Competition since 2006. It was a very comprehensive catalogue, and very complimentary.

We sold 234 cows at Crewe and I felt very sad once they had been sold and that was because of the breeding side because they were families that I had all bred and they were good cows, good consecutive cows. I was selling my bloodstock. It was a tough day for the cattle and although the sale went all right it was a long way to cart cattle; you milk them then put them on a lorry and they travel for six hours and are taken off and washed and fed; it is not good for them. The next day some of them went up to Scotland but it was pleasing for a lot of good herds to buy into them. It was sad to see them go but I found I could not sell everything; if you have a cow that is too close to calf or had just calved you are not allowed to transport them any distance so I finished up with a few left and I still have them.

That extra income from the sale of the herd at that time had to be used and we converted three barns into houses with it. We did not just spend it, we have now an income from those barns. We have reinvested it into a diversified farm business which is a leap in the right direction from the property point of view; so we leapt out of cows and into property. But for me, the biggest problem with selling the herd is that the routine you have at home goes; managing cattle is about routine and I must admit, for a day or two after the sale it felt as though a lifetime's work was being sold off.

EPILOGUE

It seems a long time ago that I used to ride around the farm on my pony called Peggy to see what was going on. It was the cart horse era, with not a tractor in sight. The quickest way to get me to understand horses was for father to buy me a pony, a nice steady docile one (which Peggy was). I rode her in gymkhanas and joined the Pony Club run by Benny Gibbs and soon realised there was more to looking after a pony – and with working horses on a farm – than I had thought. Writing this book has made me realise just what we managed to achieve; not just on the farm with our cows, or growing the business and the land we owned such as by ultimately buying the Worstead Estate but also as a community with the Worstead Festival, for example. I have met some wonderful people over my life, and had the opportunity to do a number of special and rewarding things in my time.

I look back to my earliest days on the farm and how the people I listened to as they sat around my mother and father's hearth on a Sunday afternoon was a real education to me and how I learned from them, often without realising; how being taught the bagpipes as a child led to a lifetime of pleasure and enjoyment; and the opportunities, friendships, experience and activities being a member of Aylsham Young Farmers' Club and playing a senior role in the Norfolk Federation gave me.

As the farm grew, that gave me other opportunities to travel and learn, to interact with tenants from our cottages, with other farmers, herdsmen, the people we did business with and those we competed against in the major shows as we developed our pedigree herds. It was our cows which gave us so much, not only as the mainstay of our business but also recognition across the country, particularly by winning the London Dairy Show in 1953 with Smallburgh Brenda. Thank you, Brenda, we owe you so much! That led to so many other trophies and honours over the years, notably winning the last London Dairy Show in 1970, a feat which meant that father and I, and George and Arthur Clare as herdsmen, became the only fathers and sons to achieve that. Wonderful memories. I met people through my involvement with the Holstein Society and was honoured and privileged to be President in 2004 and continue to play a role in the Norfolk group.

But when it comes to success and determination, I cannot help but be moved by what Worstead as a community achieved when it rallied round to save the village church's crumbling tower from collapse. The Worstead Festival continues to this day with its 50th anniversary in 2015 and has become a feature of the Norfolk events calendar. It not only saved the church but also raised enough money to build the village hall and enable us to donate to many other worthy causes. The way the community came together with ideas and time and effort was unbelievable and remarked upon by Her Majesty the Queen Mother when she performed the opening ceremony of the new hall in 1985. I was privileged to be chairman of Worstead Festival Committee for 39 years and during that time I also set the village up with a playing field. Though I did not expect anything like that, I was thrilled with the reaction of the village people to our efforts. Many of the people, old and young, came with good ideas and helped make the festival what it turned out to be.

It's now time to wind this up. I'd like to thank Mark Nicholls for helping me to write this book of mine with a little bit of readable patter. It is my first effort and probably the only time in my life I will write a book. I must also thank two gentlemen in Scotland who are interested in family trees – Mr Robert Currie of Strathaven and Mr William Fleming of Lanark – and some family members who nudged me in the right direction. There is also a document called Worstead Heritage Trails, which has been produced by local people and brings the village to life, with a detailed account of local history and full of many fascinating facts about Worstead. It is well worth a read. I would also like to say a big thank you to the staff we have employed on our farms over the years. They made it much easier and enjoyable for me to get away on some of my escapades.

Throughout the book, the strength of the family has been there all along. Father grew the business, often against adversity and dealing with his own health issues, and he made sure that my brother Ian and I were well-placed to take it on. He let us find our way but was always there with his advice if needed. Family, friends and relatives – and of course Marcia my wife – have been paramount in this success and I now see my family, my three boys Gavin, Alexander and Bruce, taking on the mantle as a new era in Paterson family farming begins. It is challenging times in farming today, as perhaps it has always been. But Worstead Farms Ltd is in safe hands and I see a bright future.

Gavin Alston Paterson
Church Farm, Smallburgh
April 2015

Index

Note: numbers in *italics* denote pages with pictures.